MAYENBURG: THREE PLAYS

Marius von Mayenburg

MAYENBURG: THREE PLAYS

Translated by Maja Zade

The Dog, the Night and the Knife

Eldorado

Perplex

OBERON BOOKS
LONDON

WWW.OBERONBOOKS.COM

First published in 2015 by Oberon Books Ltd
521 Caledonian Road, London N7 9RH
Tel: +44 (0) 20 7607 3637 / Fax: +44 (0) 20 7607 3629
e-mail: info@oberonbooks.com
www.oberonbooks.com

A catalogue record for this book is available from the British Library.

PB ISBN: 9781783199433
E ISBN: 9781783199440

Cover design by Tania Kelly
Robert Beyer in *Perplex* at the Schaubühne am Lehniner Platz

Contents

THE DOG, THE NIGHT AND THE KNIFE

The Dog, the Night and the Knife was first performed at the Schaubühne am Lehniner Platz on 25 May 2008, directed by Benedict Andrews.

It was first performed in the UK by Rive Productions at the Arcola Theatre on 15 September 2014, directed by Oliver Dawe.

Characters

M

THE DOGMAN / THE POLICEMAN /
THE PATIENT / THE DOCTOR / THE DOG

these five roles are played by the same actor

THE YOUNGER SISTER / THE OLDER SISTER /
THE CRIMINAL / THE LAWYER / THE NURSE

these five roles are played by the same actress

‘K. now knew that it was his duty to take the knife as it passed from hand to hand above him and plunge it into himself.’

Franz Kafka, *The Trial*

M: Last time I looked at my watch it was one thirty-eight, a hot August night. I've no idea how I got here, I had mussels for dinner, the street looks as if it's been stripped with a hoover, the plastic blinds are lowered around me, the houses are standing there with grey, closed faces reflecting the day's heat as if they had a temperature. Under a streetlamp I look at my watch, but I can't see the dial. I don't know where I am, the street is locked in a dead end, by the wall sits a box with gravel to sprinkle against the slick ice, but now it's hot. Suddenly, a man speaks behind me.

DOGMAN: Good evening.

(Nothing. The DOGMAN has a torn-off leash in his hand.)

Have you seen my dog?

M: I'm not from around here, I'm lost.

(The DOGMAN whistles.)

DOGMAN: Hear that?

(A dog howls in the distance.)

That's him. He tore himself free. This summer the wolves came deeper into the city. That's not good. It baits him.

(He whistles. The dog howls.)

He hasn't been fed for a long time, you can see the ribs under his fur. Other dogs would have gotten weak and ill, but he's getting stronger every day, his eyes flickered and his thighs quivered with anger.

(He whistles.)

M: Will you stop whistling. It's so loud.

DOGMAN: He won't hear it otherwise. Are you going to help me?

(He whistles. M covers his ears. The dog howl gets more quiet.)

He's leaving.

M: Can you tell me where we are?

DOGMAN: With pleasure, I've always been here.

(He whistles. M covers his ears. We can barely hear the dog.)

He's gone. You didn't help me. He's probably with the wolves. Once he didn't come home for several weeks and then his paw was broken and his ear torn.

(He whistles.)

M: What? Your whistling is awful.

DOGMAN: But maybe it wasn't him and I've had the wrong dog since then.

M: I want to go home.

DOGMAN: That's terrible. You're lost.

M: Where are we? I can't see any street signs.

DOGMAN: Are you on your own?

M: I had friends, we had mussels.

DOGMAN: In August?

M: But now I can't remember their faces.

DOGMAN: So no one's waiting for you?

M: Who?

DOGMAN: Not a soul.

M: Is there never a car that drives past here?

DOGMAN: And no one calls the Police.

M: Why the Police? I just want to go home.

DOGMAN: I'll help you. Step away from the streetlamp.

M: But here I can see your face better.

DOGMAN: You don't need to. I know the way.

M: You don't even know who I am.

DOGMAN: I don't need to. I've got this.

(He pulls out a long, shiny knife.)

Keep still, I'll take you home.

M: Things aren't that bad, are they?

(Tries to laugh.)

DOGMAN: My sisters are hungry.

M: Your sisters?

DOGMAN: Haven't you got any?

M: What?

DOGMAN: Any sisters?

M: Stay there.

DOGMAN: You don't need to scream. There's no one here. Everything's empty behind the blinds. There aren't even any flats. Hold still, otherwise it'll hurt.

(He strikes out at M and makes a shallow cut in his stomach.)

M: Ouch.

DOGMAN: You got scared, that's all.

M: I can barely feel the cut, but suddenly all the vessels in my body are inflamed and convulsing. I want to open my eyes but they're already open.

DOGMAN: That was clean, but not deep enough.

(He takes aim once more. M grabs his arm and takes the knife from his hand. It happens quickly and easily, without a struggle.)

M: What do you want from me?

DOGMAN: I'm hungry. I can smell your blood. I can smell your fear. You turn me on.

(He tries to hit M.)

M: Don't come any closer. I've got the knife now.

DOGMAN: That was stupid of you. A clean cut and it would have been over. Now I have to rip you apart like a wild animal. I'll push my claws into your neck.

(He tries to hit M.)

M: *(Quietly, feebly)* Help. Is anyone here.

DOGMAN: It's just me. My dog is with the wolves in the suburbs.

(The DOGMAN throws himself at M and onto the knife in M's hand. The DOGMAN hangs on M'S arm, dying.)

DOGMAN: Come morning he'll return to his bowl, which will be empty. Even before the sun rises over the estate and warms the streets again, he will have found you. He'll smell my blood flowing from your hands.

M: I didn't want this. I'll fetch a doctor.

DOGMAN: The hospital is full of sand. It blows through the broken windows, from the steppe. It crunches between the doctors' teeth, and their eyes are red. Most of them have already left for the big metropolises, the rest has dried up. Maybe one of them is taking a last stand against the desert, has locked himself in the basement and is nibbling pills.

M: You don't have to die.

DOGMAN: Yes, I do. I am. I already did. You did it.

(He stops moving.)

M: You're wrong about me, I've never killed anyone before, I'm not like that. I'll leave the knife in your stomach, it's stuck anyway. I look at my hands, but all I see is the liquid moving over them like muscular snakes. I lift my head and now a half-hidden street sign peeps out from the dry branches, and the street sign says Papegaai Straat. I'm sweating.

(We can hear wolves howling close by.)

The man is lying on the ground. I have to get away.

M: Did I wake you up?

YOUNGER SISTER: I was already awake, it's a restless night.

M: There are flowers on your dressing gown.

YOUNGER SISTER: The wolves came deeper into the city this summer.

M: I need to make a phone call.

YOUNGER SISTER: There was a fight in the street, it woke me. I think they stabbed someone.

M: That was me. It really happened.

YOUNGER SISTER: Then you did wake me up.

M: I didn't mean it.

YOUNGER SISTER: Of course. You're not like that.

M: May I use your phone to –

YOUNGER SISTER: You can hide here if you want.

M: I don't want to hide.

YOUNGER SISTER: But you have to. Otherwise they'll find you.

M: All I did was hold a knife in my hand.

YOUNGER SISTER: I believe you, but who else will? No one knows who you are. Everyone knows the Dogman.

M: Then everyone knows he and his dog go hunting under the streetlamps at night.

YOUNGER SISTER: Stay here, let the dust settle on it.

M: Dust.

YOUNGER SISTER: At least stay till dawn.

M: Are you very lonely?

YOUNGER SISTER: No, I've always been quite popular with men.

M: I like you too, but I don't want to disappear from the face of the earth, I'll call the Police.

YOUNGER SISTER: Fine, here's the phone.

M: I can't see the numbers. I try to remember the digits, but all I can think is: one, two, lost my shoe, three four, shut the door.

YOUNGER SISTER: It goes: one, two, buckle my shoe, five, six, this one sticks, eleven, twelve, dig and delve, seven eight, find a mate.

M: Not so fast. One, two, buckle my shoe, three, four –

YOUNGER SISTER: They've torn the wires from the posts anyway. Sometimes someone mends them with a pair of pliers, but most of the time they're dead. If you want the Police you'll have to go to the station.

M: How do I get there?

YOUNGER SISTER: You don't. You'll get lost.

M: But all I did was have a few mussels and now I'm standing in your blue flat and nothing's ever going to be OK again.

YOUNGER SISTER: If you want I can go instead.

M: You've only got the dressing gown.

YOUNGER SISTER: There's no one in the streets, I'll stay in the shadows, along the walls of the houses, when I have to cross the street I'll take off my shoes and walk on my feet, when a lit supermarket appears I'll cross to the other side, nothing's going to happen, why are you worrying about me?

M: Because you want to go instead of me and I don't know why.

YOUNGER SISTER: When I opened the door your outline fit the frame perfectly. The bare light bulb hung in the yellow corridor behind you, there were no snags on your figure. You would have fit into me perfectly, I knew it as soon as I saw you.

(She touches him briefly.)

But you have to watch out for my sister.

M: Your sister?

YOUNGER SISTER: She's asleep. In there.

M: So I didn't wake her up?

YOUNGER SISTER: Watch out if she does, she's not normal, she chases after every man she meets.

M: I'm not interested, I've got blood on my fingers.

YOUNGER SISTER: There's a sink.

M: I look at the water taps, but instead of hot and cold they say new and old.

YOUNGER SISTER: Don't talk to her.

M: There's sand coming out of the taps.

YOUNGER SISTER: That's the only way to get rid of the blood. If she tries to talk to you, say nothing.

M: Nothing.

YOUNGER SISTER: Don't go into her room, don't try to wake her even if she looks dead. Do nothing and nothing's going to happen.

M: Why don't you stay?

YOUNGER SISTER: Don't worry, I'll be back soon.

(She gives him a quick kiss and leaves.)

M: Of what? I look around. On the box sits a digital clock with green digits that says 'five past five'. The night feels as if this is its blackest phase, when it gets thick and syrupy, so that time drips slowly and the clock-hands get stuck, maybe a digital clock helps because it's made from light. Five past five, that's not possible, in that case I've almost made it, the sun would already have turned back and be about to reappear, do nothing and nothing will happen, half an hour later I have another look, the digital clock still says five past five, nothing's happening because I'm doing nothing, I'm standing in a strange blue flat and time and space are collapsing around me, do something and something will happen.

(He opens the bedroom door and looks inside.)

Hello?

(Nothing.)

Are you asleep or alive?

(He takes a step back.)

(The OLDER SISTER *enters from the bedroom. She's wearing a dressing gown that looks similar to her younger sister's. She looks at* M.*)*

OLDER SISTER: My sister's never done that before.

M: It's my fault –

OLDER SISTER: Brought strangers up here.

M: Because I stabbed someone.

OLDER SISTER: I know, she doesn't normally have an appetite.

M: How would you know? You were asleep.

OLDER SISTER: Very restless, in the lonely heat your body is like an animal pulling on its chain. The whistling woke me, I looked through the cracks in the blinds, I can understand my sister, you move well.

M: So you saw everything.

OLDER SISTER: I never really wake up, I sank back against my damp pillow before it was over.

M: You looked dead.

OLDER SISTER: It's the hunger. Do you work out?

M: I used to. I did rowing –

OLDER SISTER: But then the waters got more and more shallow and the crocodiles surfaced from the mud. Your front legs are still in good shape.

(She touches his arm.)

Normally my sister is shy, but for your strong hands and athletic forehead she rose above herself.

M: I didn't see her rise.

OLDER SISTER: Did you press her against the sweating wall? Our bed's in there, but she didn't want to share.

M: I don't know where you got that idea.

OLDER SISTER: Are you shy, is that why I didn't hear you moan?

M: I'm only shy with horrible people.

OLDER SISTER: Am I horrible?

M: Your sister said –

OLDER SISTER: I look exactly like her.

M: That's right. As soon as I saw you I thought –

OLDER SISTER: Exactly, we're from the same egg, in mother's womb I pushed my feet in her face, she was so weak they almost forgot all about her, I grabbed her hair and took her with me.

M: She warned me about you.

OLDER SISTER: Because she knows what I get up to. Because she knows I expose my back, that's bold, turning my back on a stranger, a stranger who's still got blood dripping from his fingers, turning my back on him, letting my dressing gown slide from my shoulders to where the downy hair grows in the shadow, exposing my back, which is flawless and the same colour all over, transparent and shimmering and cast from one piece, so firm and soft that you want to stick out your tongue and lick along its smooth surface from the downy hair to my neck and breathe in the exhilarating smell of heat, intoxicated because none of the hairs resist and because my whole body moves under your tongue and strains towards you, my sister knows you'll be mine then, that from then on you'll only think within the bounds of my body and that soon your whole being will circulate in my bloodstream, molecule by molecule, body and soul.

(She returns to the bedroom. While she's walking she slowly lets the dressing gown slide from her shoulders.)

M: Her back glows although there's no moon. I look at the clock again, it shines green in the room and still says five past five.

(He follows her.)

(M enters from the bedroom, in tatters. He covers his mouth.)

M: You bit my tongue.

(The OLDER SISTER follows him from the bedroom.)

OLDER SISTER: And touched the cut in your stomach with my fingers, I know. I wanted to see if you'd moan.

M: I wonder where your sister is. My tongue's bleeding.

OLDER SISTER: Am I supposed to be sorry?

M: I've never experienced this kind of greed.

OLDER SISTER: It has nothing to do with you, it's the hunger.

M: Have you had enough?

OLDER SISTER: I haven't finished.

(She holds a long, shiny knife in her hand, it's the same one that the DOGMAN used.)

M: Put that away, I've got a bad feeling about long knives.

OLDER SISTER: Not very gallant, all this whining about a bit of blood, as if it hadn't been worth it.

M: No, it was, definitely, every drop.

OLDER SISTER: I don't kiss everyone, you know.

M: And it was very nice.

OLDER SISTER: Very nice, yes, but now I'm afraid I have to kill you.

M: I turn round and tear the door open but outside, where the yellow staircase used to be is a wardrobe that shimmers white like bones.

OLDER SISTER: This isn't revenge, okay.

M: For what? I didn't hurt you.

OLDER SISTER: We kept telling him, sooner or later, when you're down there walking the dog, someone's going to take your knife and pin you to the grass like a butterfly. But what brother listens to his sisters?

M: That was your brother, the Dogman?

OLDER SISTER: I don't care about my brother, I want to eat your flesh. If you keep still it won't be unpleasant. I know cuts –

(She has approached him and strikes out at him. M catches her hand, with a lurch the knife enters her stomach, easily, without a struggle.)

OLDER SISTER: Aha.

M: I didn't mean it.

OLDER SISTER: Hold me?

M: I'd rather stand here.

OLDER SISTER: That's it, I'll stop now, everything's gone to the devil.

(M holds her.)

What you're holding in your arms, this flawless, smooth, beautiful body I've been feeding for years, gone to the devil because of a hole in my stomach, a few silly centimetres.

M: I'm sorry.

OLDER SISTER: Easy for you to say, you've no idea how desperate you'll be for a kiss from me, no matter how bloody, when you hobble over the steppe under a cold moon poisoned, hunted and chivvied, hungry and sleepless, and howl after the wolves because you can't chase the memory of me from your body and you think someone has cast an evil shadow over your life, but in the blazing light, when the sun scorches you, you'll realise that you're the shadow, because it's dark in your body unless you take a knife and cut a window into it and let the light in between your organs, and you'll long for my expert cut to take away the gloomy shadow and free you, but of course it'll be too late then.

(She stops moving.)

M: Don't look at me with your dead eyes, that's not me, I feel as if I'm the thought of someone dreams hard and sweats, or the failed joke of a drunk man. Where to?

(He drags her into the bedroom.)

That's where she was lying before sleeping like a dead woman, now she's a dead woman lying there as if she's asleep.

(He returns.)

My forehead is damp and cold, I look back at the digital clock whose green digits are surprisingly bright, the clock still says five past five, but this time I take a closer look and realise the digits don't tell the time, the clock says S.O.S., says it loud and clear, the digits say S.O.S., five, zero, five, save our souls. I need to get out of here.

(The YOUNGER SISTER enters from the bedroom, she's accompanied by a Policeman.)

YOUNGER SISTER: *(To M.)* I told you not to speak to her.

POLICEMAN: I'm confused.

YOUNGER SISTER: And to do nothing, and now you've gone and done something.

M: She looked dead, like someone who needed to be saved.

POLICEMAN: *(To the YOUNGER SISTER.)* You said it was about the man with the torn-off leash lying down there, among the bushes.

YOUNGER SISTER: Exactly, with a hole in his stomach.

POLICEMAN: But now you take me to your bedroom and there's a woman lying there.

M: *(To the POLICEMAN.)* Do I know you? Your face looks familiar.

POLICEMAN: Did you stab the dogman?

M: I can't remember. Now it feels as if I'd just seen him step through this door.

POLICEMAN: Did you have a bad childhood? Something that would explain your aggression?

YOUNGER SISTER: He's not aggressive.

M: I can't remember my childhood.

POLICEMAN: *(To the YOUNGER SISTER.)* Can't remember: a trauma.

M: Isn't that true of everyone? Childhood was such a long time ago.

POLICEMAN: *(To M.)* Good for you, it explains your aggression.

YOUNGER SISTER: He's not aggressive, the other one attacked *him.*

POLICEMAN: The other one?

M: Her sister was watching through the blinds.

YOUNGER SISTER: You shouldn't have woken her up.

POLICEMAN: It's all the same now, she can't testify to anything.

(He picks up the knife and examines it.)

M: I'm sorry that was your brother –

YOUNGER SISTER: Me too. You weren't supposed to know. My embarrassing siblings.

POLICEMAN: Who does this pretty knife belong to?

M: The brother.

YOUNGER SISTER: The sister.

M: Why do you ask? Weren't you there?

POLICEMAN: And he wanted to butcher you?

M: He even slashed me.

(He shows his wound.)

POLICEMAN: Not deep enough. Be careful it doesn't get infected. Does it hurt?

M: Yes, now that you're looking at it, it started. It's bleeding again.

(The POLICEMAN matches the cut to the knife.)

POLICEMAN: The cut was made with the same weapon. It's a clear case of self-defence.

YOUNGER SISTER: Like I said, he's innocent.

POLICEMAN: You're innocent.

M: And the woman?

POLICEMAN: Is his sister, you're free to go wherever you want.

M: I can go?

POLICEMAN: Wherever you want.

M: But I don't want to. I'm scared.

YOUNGER SISTER: Stay here.

POLICEMAN: Go home.

M: I don't know where that is, or where I am.

YOUNGER SISTER: Papegaai Straat.

POLICEMAN: You can come to the station with me and sleep for a few hours until dawn.

YOUNGER SISTER: Don't do it.

POLICEMAN: I'll give you a blanket.

YOUNGER SISTER: You'd better stay here.

POLICEMAN: *(To M.)* Only if you want.

M: I can't stay here.

YOUNGER SISTER: Don't go with the Policeman. Please. Stay with me.

M: Forget about me. I ruined my life tonight, it'll never heal. You have a lovely face, but do you really want to look at me? Find yourself a nice young man or buy yourself a dog.

YOUNGER SISTER: You don't have to get harsh with me.

M: That wasn't harsh.

POLICEMAN: I'm ready.

M: I look at the green digits. I have to get out of here.

(He leaves the flat with the POLICEMAN.*)*

POLICEMAN: So where did his dog go?

M: His dog is with the wolves.

(They've gone.)

YOUNGER SISTER: Don't go to the station, they've got washable walls and basements full of corpses. Stay with me.

POLICEMAN: You can rest in here.

M: But that looks like –

POLICEMAN: I'll leave the door open. Just so you have somewhere to sleep.

M: It's a cell.

POLICEMAN: Yes, sorry, that's all I've got, I'm afraid this isn't a hotel.

M: Did someone wait for his execution in here?

POLICEMAN: They used to do them in the courtyard, in front of this window. Why?

M: It smells like it.

POLICEMAN: I hope you don't mind sleeping on the bed springs, we had to burn the mattress.

(Because M is staring at a bucket.)

You won't need the bucket. You can use the toilet behind the guardroom. The door stays open.

M: Thanks.

POLICEMAN: That's what we're here for.

(He leaves and locks the door.)

M: Stop! What are you doing?

(The POLICEMAN unlocks it.)

POLICEMAN: Yes, what is it?

M: You just locked the door.

POLICEMAN: Did I? Old habits. I'm sorry. Of course the door stays open, you're not a prisoner.

(He leaves.)

M: I peer through the bright crack in the door, the Policeman is sitting on the table combing a wig, or maybe he's stroking a child, I'm too tired, the cut's throbbing, my eyes roll backwards, I fall asleep.

(The POLICEMAN pushes the CRIMINAL into the room.)

CRIMINAL: Excuse me for living.

POLICEMAN: You've said enough.

CRIMINAL: Why don't you just break my legs?

POLICEMAN: You're not going to do any more running. I'm locking you up.

M: Hang on, not in here.

CRIMINAL: *(To the POLICEMAN.)* You've taken me out of context, if someone did that to you they'd have to lock you up too.

POLICEMAN: *(To the CRIMINAL.)* I'll slap your mouth shut if you keep talking.

M: Not in here with me.

POLICEMAN: Who's chattering now?

M: I'm not a prisoner.

POLICEMAN: What do you want?

CRIMINAL: What does he want?

M: You can't lock him up in here.

POLICEMAN: On the contrary, that's what I'm in the middle of.

M: Then let me go first.

POLICEMAN: Where do you want to go?

M: Back to Papegaai Straat.

POLICEMAN: You're staying put.

CRIMINAL: Exactly, otherwise I'll get lonely.

M: I'm only here so I can get some sleep, don't you remember?

POLICEMAN: You've been in this cell for years, and every time you tell me a different story. I'm sick of your games. You think I don't have a soul just because I work here. Aren't you ashamed of yourself?

M: I've only just – you're confusing me with someone else.

POLICEMAN: Right, because you look confusingly similar.

M: I'm not a criminal, you don't need to lock me up.

POLICEMAN: Then what are you doing in here?

M: Don't you recognise me? Look at me.

(The POLICEMAN looks at him.)

POLICEMAN: You don't look particularly unusual.

(He turns to leave.)

M: You can't lock me up with this criminal.

POLICEMAN: But I'm locking this criminal up with you.

(He leaves and locks the door from outside.)

M: Do we need to decide who's on top and who's on the bottom?

CRIMINAL: Both can be nice, I don't really have a preference.

M: I've never been to prison before.

CRIMINAL: You can ask me why I'm here.

M: What did you do?

CRIMINAL: I did things with people.

M: With people?

CRIMINAL: With animals, with people, if that's how you want to put it.

M: Animals.

CRIMINAL: If you want.

M: I don't need to hear this, I'll only get scared.

CRIMINAL: If that's the only thing that scares you.

(Nothing.)

M: What did you mean when you said you don't really have a preference?

CRIMINAL: What?

M: When I asked about the bunk bed. About who's on top and who's on the bottom.

CRIMINAL: I've no idea what you're talking about.

(Nothing. M looks at the CRIMINAL.)

M: Do you know me?

CRIMINAL: No.

M: Don't you have the feeling that we've met?

CRIMINAL: Isn't that what you say when you want to sleep with a woman?

M: I've seen your face before.

CRIMINAL: Is that what you want?

M: I'm not sure, but it was a bit different.

CRIMINAL: Are you sure that's what you want?

M: It felt a bit different to look at you.

CRIMINAL: You can have that if you want.

M: It felt different.

CRIMINAL: Maybe it felt like this?

(He kisses him. M doesn't struggle. While they're kissing the door opens and the POLICEMAN enters without them noticing.)

M: Who are you?

CRIMINAL: I'm your lawyer.

M: I don't have a lawyer.

CRIMINAL: *(Now LAWYER.)* Me.

M: But you're a criminal.

LAWYER: That's irrelevant.

M: Irrelevant to what?

LAWYER: We haven't got much time, they want to carry out the sentence before dawn.

M: There is no sentence, there aren't even any charges, I'm innocent.

LAWYER: You don't have to show off with me. I'm your lawyer.

M: I've only been here an hour, I'm only here to sleep, I haven't even been arrested.

LAWYER: Trust me, the enamel bowl for the execution is sitting in the yard.

M: The execution?

LAWYER: What did you think? That they'd put a cart with eight goats in the yard, decorate it with flower garlands, and when you say goodbye the other prisoners wave and throw flower blossoms while you roll through the steel gates and into the steppe? If we want to reopen your case we need to hurry, the sky won't stay black for long.

POLICEMAN: Time's up, you have to go.

LAWYER: We're just getting started.

POLICEMAN: I don't care if you use the brief time allotted to you for your case or the exchange of human warmth, but don't blame me if you end up running out of time. I didn't get you into this mess, I'd rather be somewhere else myself, but since people like you exist I have to spend my time in this place, at least forty years, no criminal stays here that long, and I didn't commit a crime.

M: Neither did I.

POLICEMAN: *(To the LAWYER.)* I have to ask you to leave, the delinquent is expecting a visitor.

M: I'm not expecting any visitors.

POLICEMAN: A visitor with pale skin.

LAWYER: If it's that important to you.

M: To me?

LAWYER: Maybe your visitor can stay the execution.

M: But no one knows I'm here.

POLICEMAN: A lady.

LAWYER: I think you're being hasty. There is still an – admittedly slight – hope of staying the execution, maybe even of preventing it. But of course you're free to waste this opportunity, to proceed directly to the last wishes and call the ladies.

M: I didn't call anyone.

LAWYER: You'll think of me before the first rays of sun brighten the horizon and they lead you into the yard and you shiver.

(The LAWYER leaves.)

M: Wait.

POLICEMAN: He'll be back.

(M doubles over.)

Are you looking for something?

M: The cut.

POLICEMAN: What?

M: The cut in my stomach.

(The POLICEMAN examines him.)

POLICEMAN: Not deep enough.

M: I need a doctor.

POLICEMAN: It'll sort itself out before sunrise.

M: No need to demoralize me. I'll tell you everything you want to know.

POLICEMAN: What was the liquid in the glass capsules my mother kept in her desk?

M: How should I know?

POLICEMAN: Exactly, how would you know?

M: I can only tell you things about me.

POLICEMAN: Go on.

M: What?

POLICEMAN: See, you're stubborn.

M: Ask me something.

POLICEMAN: Why did you do it?

M: What? What did I do?

POLICEMAN: Difficult. You're being difficult. I'm doing everything I can, but you're being difficult. I'm wasting my time.

M: Wait.

POLICEMAN: Maybe you were hungry?

M: No, I had mussels.

POLICEMAN: In August?

M: A large plastic bag, I really wasn't hungry after that.

POLICEMAN: Then why did you do it?

M: I don't know.

POLICEMAN: If you think being obstinate helps.

M: I really don't know.

POLICEMAN: So no motive. Lechery. Psychopath. That's the end of you.

(He turns to go.)

M: Wait.

(The POLICEMAN stops.)

Did you ever have a dog?

POLICEMAN: We don't have dogs here.

M: I knew someone who did.

POLICEMAN: Not for a long time.

M: But this man –

POLICEMAN: We ate the dogs.

(He turns to go.)

I'll send the lady in now.

(He leaves. The YOUNGER SISTER enters.)

YOUNGER SISTER: You look terrible.

M: You don't.

YOUNGER SISTER: I saw an enamel bowl when I crossed the yard.

M: It's for me.

YOUNGER SISTER: I was afraid of that.

M: You were right, I shouldn't have come here.

YOUNGER SISTER: Too late now.

M: I'd forgotten all about you.

YOUNGER SISTER: Is that why you didn't answer my letters?

M: Letters?

YOUNGER SISTER: I wrote to you every day.

M: I didn't get anything. But I've only been here one night.

YOUNGER SISTER: I didn't know your name, maybe they threw the letters away.

M: My name is – I think about it, but all I can come up with are the names of wild cats, as if their screams are louder and drown out my stupid name, leopard, lion, panther, jaguar, lynx –

YOUNGER SISTER: I'm alone a lot of the time now. My brother is dead and so is my sister, you know?

M: Are you trying to torture me, is that why you're here?

YOUNGER SISTER: You're the last man I knew, I want to warn you.

M: It can't get much worse than this, can it?

YOUNGER SISTER: You mustn't fight.

M: They'll kill me anyway, I'd rather fight than go like an animal to the slaughter.

YOUNGER SISTER: If you fight they'll do it here and now. And then I can't help you.

M: What do you want me for? I'm embarrassing, no one wants to be in the same room as me, people avoid me like a patient about to die.

YOUNGER SISTER: I want to be with you, I'm sure it's terribly lonely next to a body you've killed. I'm sure if I can fill your loneliness my life will be heroic. As long as you don't struggle and ruin everything.

M: Then I won't fight.

YOUNGER SISTER: Do nothing and nothing's going to happen.

M: Nothing at all?

YOUNGER SISTER: Think of me.

(She turns to go.)

M: I don't terrify you?

YOUNGER SISTER: No. Not at all. Look at the sky, it'll calm you. The grand order up there, at night.

(She's gone.)

M: There's a narrow window underneath the ceiling, but there's no order. The sky's a cage full of panicking birds.

(The POLICEMAN enters.)

POLICEMAN: Someone delivered this for you.

(Hands him a small parcel wrapped in brown paper.)

M: Who?

POLICEMAN: I don't know him.

M: A man?

POLICEMAN: With a torn-off rope in his hand.

M: I look at my watch, but now there are two clips attached to my leather bracelet, they're holding an operated frog that gives off flames.

(To the POLICEMAN.) How much time do I have left?

POLICEMAN: Not much. A couple of minutes.

M: And then? Everything's supposed to carry on without me?

POLICEMAN: What do you mean everything? There's not much happening here anyway.

M: Have you ever pictured it?

POLICEMAN: What?

M: That the world carries on without you? The endless time afterwards that takes place without you?

POLICEMAN: I don't have to picture anything, this isn't about me, it's about you. I'll stay here and watch you leave the world. Like that. Not the other way round.

M: First there's you and me and then you're suddenly on your own.

POLICEMAN: Do you want to have a wash? I can get you some water and a bar of soap. Otherwise we'll do it afterwards.

M: You don't need to wash me, I'll end up in the ground anyway.

POLICEMAN: No.

M: I won't?

POLICEMAN: No. Everyone here is really hungry.

M: What do you mean?

POLICEMAN: Me, for example. I'm really hungry too.

(The LAWYER returns.)

LAWYER: Don't you want to see what's in the parcel?

M: What do you mean, really hungry?

POLICEMAN: Stop making such a fuss. You'll be dead.

M: No.

LAWYER: Open the parcel.

POLICEMAN: So you don't want to wash?

M: I refuse.

POLICEMAN: Then get ready. The sky above the steppe is about to turn pink.

M: Don't touch me.

(The LAWYER takes the parcel and rips it open.)

POLICEMAN: It won't hurt, I've been trained, a clean cut and it's over, you won't suffer.

M: No, definitely not.

(The LAWYER has pulled a long knife from the parcel. The same as in the dead end and the sisters' flat.)

POLICEMAN: If you fight me I'll do it here and now and it'll take a long time and every stab will hurt.

(The LAWYER hands M the knife. M stabs him at once.)

LAWYER: Good. That's good.

POLICEMAN: Aha.

M: What?

POLICEMAN: The cut in your stomach will swell up into red lips that denounce against you and laugh at you, and the mouth will open and swallow you up.

LAWYER: Stab him again.

(M stabs the POLICEMAN again.)

POLICEMAN: Yes.

(He stops moving.)

M: The sky looks as if someone had knocked something over. I wasn't supposed to fight back.

LAWYER: Then you'd be hanging over the bowl out there with your throat slit open.

M: He was alive just now.

LAWYER: We have to get out of here.

M. Stopped talking.

LAWYER: Come on. Let's go.

(M doubles over.)

M: The cut hurts, I can't walk.

LAWYER: I'll help you.

(M leans on the LAWYER. They start to leave.)

M: Did he just laugh?

LAWYER: Who?

M: The Policeman. I thought I just heard him laugh.

LAWYER: Pity we have to leave him like this.

M: I turn around, but there's nothing left. Everything closes behind me, I'm gliding through black water. It's over.

(They've gone.)

(The LAWYER is helping M. A PATIENT is sitting in the shadow waiting, M doesn't notice him.)

M: Thank you.

LAWYER: That's all right.

M: You can barely stand up yourself.

LAWYER: I'm just hungry.

PATIENT: Good evening.

(M, panicking, points the knife at the PATIENT.)

M: Who are you, what do you want?

PATIENT: I was here first. I'm waiting.

M: Why are you talking to me?

PATIENT: There's only one doctor on night duty, with one sister. They're very busy.

LAWYER: Why not give me the knife?

M: Why?

LAWYER: Before there's an accident.

M: That man does not need to talk to me.

LAWYER: He's just sitting there waiting.

PATIENT: Since midnight.

M: He said good evening.

PATIENT: I don't like people jumping the queue.

LAWYER: You're nervous, give me the knife.

M: But keep an eye on him.

(He hands him the knife. The LAWYER takes it and looks at it.)

LAWYER: Nice. Just before, I thought I'd seen one just like this.

M: Aha.

LAWYER: Very nice, the knife.

(He looks at M. Nothing.)

M: Why are you staring at me?

LAWYER: Look. I'm hungry.

M: So?

LAWYER: I wouldn't need to kill you. A leg, maybe just an arm would be –

M: Pardon?

LAWYER: I'm not like the others. I saved your life.
But you need to understand that I'm hungry.

M: You want to cut one of my legs off.

LAWYER: An arm might be enough for now.

M: An arm?

LAWYER: Yes. There *are* people with only one arm. Some of them are even married. Hold still.

(The PATIENT watches with interest.)

M: Wait.

LAWYER: But not for long, I'm really hungry.

M: You remind me of someone.

LAWYER: Who?

M: Yes, now that the knife is in your hand, I know that face. Although it was different.

LAWYER: Different how?

M: Sorry.

LAWYER: Yes?

M: May I?

LAWYER: What?

M: I think it was more like this.

(He kisses him. The LAWYER doesn't fight him. While he kisses him, M effortlessly takes the knife from his hand and stabs him in the side. The PATIENT watches with interest but doesn't move.)

LAWYER: A face like this?

M: Sorry.

LAWYER: Why are you doing this? I saved you.

M: *(To the LAWYER.)* I can still save you as well.

(Shouts.) Doctor.

(Static noise from the intercom.)

M: *(To the PATIENT.)* Help me, we have to take him inside.

(He drags the LAWYER towards the door.)

LAWYER: Not the doctor.

PATIENT: I'm next, I'm not leaving here.

LAWYER: I only wanted your arm.

M: I can't, not without my arm.

LAWYER: And I have to die.

M: No, we're at the hospital.

(Shouts.) Doctor!

LAWYER: I don't want a doctor!

M: *(To the PATIENT.)* Please help me.

PATIENT: You think he's going to die?

M: If you don't help us.

(The PATIENT leans back. M drags the lawyer through the door.)

LAWYER: Please don't.

(They're outside.)

PATIENT: He doesn't want to. He's scared.

(Noise from the intercom.)

(M returns.)

M: The doctor's looking after him now.

PATIENT: That's great.

M: I'm sorry, now you've got a longer wait.

PATIENT: On the contrary.

M: What's wrong with you?

PATIENT: I'm hungry.

M: That's no reason to go and see a doctor.

PATIENT: It's the only place where they occasionally have something.

M: Here?

PATIENT: Occasionally they still get something in.

M: Aha.

PATIENT: Aren't you hungry?

M: No, I had mussels.

PATIENT: In August?

M: I was with friends, the mosquitoes sucked us dry.

PATIENT: They haven't got anything at the moment. The cooling chambers are empty.

M: You think they'll get something tonight?

PATIENT: How ill are you?

M: I've got a cut in my stomach.

PATIENT: Can I have a look?

M: You?

PATIENT: I've seen lots of cuts.

M: *(Shows him his cut.)*

PATIENT: *(Disappointed)* It's not deep enough. You don't have to be scared.

M: But it hurts.

PATIENT: *(Not interested)* Yes yes, that hurts.

(The NURSE enters.)

NURSE: Next, please.

M: Oh.

PATIENT: Me. I'm next.

M: *(To the NURSE.)* Who are you?

PATIENT: That's the nurse, isn't that obvious.

M: I've seen you before.

NURSE: What's wrong with you?

M: Me?

NURSE: Seeing as you're staring at me.

M: Nothing, nothing's wrong with me, nothing.

NURSE: Then what are you doing here?

M: I –

PATIENT: Nothing's wrong with him, it's my turn.

M: My friend. How is my friend?

NURSE: Who?

M: I just took him inside.

PATIENT: He stabbed him.

NURSE: We're taking care of him.

M: Then he's no longer in pain?

NURSE: Definitely not.

M: Good.

PATIENT: And what about me?

NURSE: What about you?

PATIENT: Hungry. I'm hungry.

NURSE: Yes. Come. We have something for you now. You can go inside.

(The PATIENT steps through the door.)

M: And I was sure –

NURSE: What's wrong with you?

M: With me? Why?

NURSE: I can smell it.

M: What?

NURSE: Your blood.

M: I – oh, that. It's just a cut.

NURSE: From a knife.

M: Exactly, but –

NURSE: Can I have a look?

M: Of course, I mean – you work here.

(He shows her the cut.)

NURSE: That's beautiful.

M: Beautiful?

NURSE: A clean cut. Like a mouth with moist lips.

M: He tried to slit me open.

NURSE: Does it hurt?

M: No, not – yes, now that you're looking at it.

NURSE: Someone should have taken care of this ages ago.

M: And now it's bleeding again.

NURSE: Wait.

(She looks at the cut close up, breathes in with closed eyes, can't control herself and starts to lick the wound.)

M: Oh. Is that the –

(The NURSE briefly looks up.)

NURSE: What?

M: The correct method?

NURSE: Do you know a better one?

(She keeps licking.)

M: No, I – I'm not a doctor.

DOCTOR: *(A voice on the intercom.)* Sister?

(M looks up. The NURSE doesn't hear anything.)

Sister?

M: I think you're wanted.

(The NURSE looks up.)

DOCTOR: Sister, can you hear me?

NURSE: Yes, doctor.

DOCTOR: What are you doing, sister?

NURSE: Nothing.

DOCTOR: What's taking you so long?

NURSE: There's another patient here.

DOCTOR: Another patient?

NURSE: An injured man.

DOCTOR: The one that was in such a state?

NURSE: He's been cut.

DOCTOR: Leave the man alone.

NURSE: He's bleeding.

DOCTOR: He injured his friend very badly. We need you here to finish this.

NURSE: I'll be right with you.

(She stands up.)

M: Look at me.

NURSE: What?

M: Did you look at my face?

NURSE: We don't know each other.

M: You have one green eye and one red.

NURSE: It just looks like it. Wait here until we call you.

(She exits through the door.)

DOCTOR: *(Voice on the intercom.)* Stop pulling a face.

M: Me? What? Who –

DOCTOR: I know what you're thinking.

M: You mean because I – why, what face?

DOCTOR: Large quantities of hot secretions have discharged themselves into your body and now they're circulating in your veins, causing a frenzied, heavy-lidded descent into boundless orgies of the brain during which your body can harden like a bronze statue that sounds like a bell when you touch it and later melts in a blazing heat, dissolves and vanishes. And you think this growth of sexual lust is caused by the actions of the sister who looked after your wound, and that there's a special bond between you, but although the sister's ability to plunge ordered organisms into chaos is proven to be above average –

M: What are you trying to tell me?

DOCTOR: You're confusing the person of the sister with your body's own cause-and-effect mechanism.

(Static noise.)

M: You're jealous.

DOCTOR: I'm what?

M: You want her and now you're jealous.

DOCTOR: Of what? The pitiful condition you're in? The fidgety lust in your…

(Static noise.)

…in no way due to the stimulation of…

(Static.)

M: Pardon?

DOCTOR: *(Interrupted by static noise)* …manifests the first signs of a romantic emotional confusion… nothing but the triumph of a chemical process… failure-embracing controlling processes of human intelligence… longing to succumb, unconditionally conquered… drown… flood of manipulative bodily fluids…

(A whistle, the connection is broken.)

M: Hello? Hello? I didn't get the last bit. Hello?

(The POLICEMAN enters.)

POLICEMAN: Are you the man that stabbed someone?

M: You were lying in your own blood just now.

POLICEMAN: Me?

M: I stabbed you with this knife.

POLICEMAN: You've got some funny ideas. Give me the knife.

M: No. I'm holding onto it now.

POLICEMAN: The thing I don't get is: you can't really think you're going to get away, you're leaving a smoking trail of blood behind you.

M: That's my blood seeping out of my wound.

POLICEMAN: But one day you'll stand in front of the judge and he'll send you to the devil.

M: Then I'll stab him, and the devil as well.

POLICEMAN: Give me the knife.

M: There.

(He stabs him. The POLICEMAN laughs.)

POLICEMAN: You got the right man.

(He staggers towards the door, collapses on the doorstep and falls out of the room. The door closes behind him. Static noise from the intercom.)

(The YOUNGER SISTER enters.)

YOUNGER SISTER: There you are.

M: Weren't you in – just now – no?

YOUNGER SISTER: We have to get out of here at once, this is a bad place.

M: You're – no, you're not, but your eyes –

YOUNGER SISTER: We have to escape. Out of town and into the steppe.

M: I can't leave here.

YOUNGER SISTER: Then things are going to get bad.

M: My lawyer is in there, I stabbed him.

YOUNGER SISTER: He's not there any more, trust me.

M: What?

YOUNGER SISTER: If you wait too long it'll descend on you.

M: What's going to descend on whom?

YOUNGER SISTER: Can't you feel the night sucking at you, the sky swooping down to breathe you in, the ground racing under your feet? If you stay you won't make it till dawn.

M: I won't make it anyway, my wound is infected, I can't walk upright.

YOUNGER SISTER: You can lean on me.

M: There are people here that can help me.

YOUNGER SISTER: No here one is going to help you.

M: This is the sickroom.

YOUNGER SISTER: No, it's the sick room, that's what the flickering neon letters by the entrance say, because it's true: only sick people work here, who's going to help you?

M: The sister has already helped me.

YOUNGER SISTER: The sister? I warned you about the sister.

M: What?

YOUNGER SISTER: Is she here?

M: Who? Yes, she works here.

YOUNGER SISTER: Then I have to go now. I can't be in the same place as her.

M: I don't understand –

YOUNGER SISTER: Are you coming?

M: Where? No.

YOUNGER SISTER: You've fallen under her spell.

M: She took care of my wound, that's all.

YOUNGER SISTER: I bet she did. Please come with me. I know you've been infected, that you don't want to tear yourself away from her body, they all felt that way, but have a look in the rubbish bags in the skips in the yard.

M: What's in there?

YOUNGER SISTER: Come and have a look.

M. I don't want to go into the yard, the light's orange, the air is stale and thousands of shiny green flies are hovering over the skips.

(A whistle on the intercom. It sounds like the DOGMAN's whistle in the dead end.)

YOUNGER SISTER: They know I'm here.

M: Who?

YOUNGER SISTER: Come on.

(She grabs him and tries to pull him with her. He's holding the knife.)

M: Let go of me.

YOUNGER SISTER: You're going to die.

M: So are you if you don't let go at once.

(A whistle on the intercom. She lets him go.)

DOCTOR: *(A voice on the intercom, with static noise.)* …aggregates have failed… storage rooms… barbed wire.

YOUNGER SISTER: Good luck then.

(She gives him a quick kiss and is gone.)

(M touches his mouth.)

M: Sand.

(He spits.)

There's sand in my mouth, on my tongue, on my teeth –

(He spits.)

I swallow –

(He swallows.)

Swallow the sand, and I see it trickling from the air vents at the back, whirling veils in front of the neon pipes, and now –

(He touches his neck.)

Now it's everywhere, at the back of my neck, under my arms, in my eyes, I can't see anything, now I can't see anything, between my legs –

(He puts his hand in his trousers.)

(The DOCTOR enters. He wipes his mouth with a towel and throws it away.)

DOCTOR: Very good.

(The sandattack is over.)

M: What's very good?

DOCTOR: I see you've brought your own instruments.

(He burps.)

Excuse me.

M: What instruments?

DOCTOR: Let's have a look at your wound.

M: Here.

(He shows him his wound.)

DOCTOR: Nice.

M: Where's the sister?

DOCTOR: I'm sure you can wait. We had a big operation in there, she's still cleaning up.

M: How is he?

DOCTOR: The worst is behind him. Does that hurt?

M: Can I see him? I'd like to know how he is.

DOCTOR: He's not here anymore.

M: I didn't see him come out.

DOCTOR: He took the back door to the yard.

M: Ouch!

DOCTOR: So that hurts. Good.

M: What's good about it?

(The DOCTOR has finished the examination and is wiping his hands.)

DOCTOR: You have a cut going from left to right, inflicted with a sharp blade.

M: I know.

DOCTOR: What did he want to extract?

M: Pardon?

DOCTOR: Why did he need this opening in your stomach?

M: I don't know.

DOCTOR: You don't know.

M: I thought he wanted to eat me.

DOCTOR: Do you want to get better or not?

M: Of course.

DOCTOR: Then you'll have to answer my questions honestly.

M: I've no idea what he wanted.

DOCTOR: There's something in there.

M: No.

DOCTOR: Something he wanted.

M: No.

DOCTOR: But I can still see the scar from the opening where they inserted the object.

M: What scar?

DOCTOR: Here.

(Roughly pulls up his shirt, shows him.)

M: That's my belly button.

DOCTOR: Your what?

M: Belly button.

DOCTOR: That word doesn't exist.

M: Yes it does. Belly button.

DOCTOR: Are you listening to yourself? Belly button.

M: Everyone has a belly button.

DOCTOR: I'd know, I'm a doctor, I see lots of naked people, but none of them has such an original scar. They inserted something right there.

M: You've got a belly button as well.

DOCTOR: No.

M: Yes.

DOCTOR: No.

(He pulls up his shirt.)

Where?

(No navel.)

So, what have you got in there?

M: But that's –

DOCTOR: Let's have a look. Sister!

NURSE: *(A voice on the intercom.)* Yes, doctor.

DOCTOR: Please come here, we need to operate.

NURSE: Yes, Sir.

DOCTOR: Bring the instruments.

NURSE: Yes, sir.

M: I don't want an operation.

DOCTOR: No one wants an operation. But sometimes it's necessary.

M: But it's *not* necessary. I just want you to fix the cut. I don't want a new cut.

DOCTOR: But this cut was made by an amateur. I can do better than that.

(The NURSE enters.)

M: Help me.

NURSE: With pleasure.

M: He wants to operate.

NURSE: You'll get a shot, then you won't feel anything.

M: I don't want a shot.

NURSE: Yes, you want a shot.

(She has a syringe in her hand. She and the DOCTOR start to drive M into a corner.)

M: What are those spots on your apron?

NURSE: Keep calm, it's only coffee.

M: So red? Such red coffee?

DOCTOR: *(To the NURSE.)* I'm sorry, you've cleaned everything, now it'll get dirty again.

NURSE: My mistake, I should have guessed we'd need it again.

M: What? What do you need?

DOCTOR: Hold still, it's pointless anyway. There's two of us and you're on your own.

(He tries to grab M, who stabs him with the knife. The DOCTOR stumbles.)

No, the other way round, we're doing the cutting, not you, take it out, what an amateur, the knife, but deep, hah, everything, everything out, all the heat out through this tiny amateur cut, there's a cold draft, so cold, hah, light, very light and cold.

(He stops moving.)

NURSE: Why don't you just lie down? And then we'll take care of your wound? Like before? Wasn't that nice?

M: Yes. No.

(He stabs her.)

NURSE: Two at the same time, that hungry.

M: I'm not hungry.

NURSE: Don't leave me here, it would be a waste.

M: I had mussels.

NURSE: In August.

(She stops moving.)

M: And now? You've stopped talking? Anything else? Anyone else? Anyone still hungry? Come on out, get out of your holes, come and get me, crawl out from under the lino, rain black from the sprinklers, turn to smoke and seep from the sockets, I'll butcher you, all of you, I've got the knife and you don't, if there's someone who hasn't had enough, I've got plenty left, bastards, I feel awful.

(Static noise from the intercom. He exits through the door.)

(The YOUNGER SISTER is propping up M, who is in terrible pain.)

M: I can't walk anymore.

YOUNGER SISTER: Then we'll have a short rest.

M: And then? Keep running until we collapse? I'm collapsing already.

YOUNGER SISTER: I'll help you.

M: A short rest is not enough. I need a long rest.

YOUNGER SISTER: Then they'll get us. You lost a lot of blood along the way, they're following the trail.

M: Let them find me. The moon hangs cold over the steppe, a large blind eye, the sky has come down low, the horizon starts here, in front of my feet, and moves away with each step.

YOUNGER SISTER: Hear that?

M: What?

(In the distance wolves are howling, like in the dead end.)

YOUNGER SISTER: The wolves. We got too close. They've picked up our scent. We need to get going.

M: Let them come.

YOUNGER SISTER: Do you want the wolves to eat me?

M: I wasn't thinking about you.

YOUNGER SISTER: Why not?

M: I keep getting weaker and my wound hurts, that's all I can think about.

YOUNGER SISTER: You only need to keep going till morning.

M: I'm scared that some of this night will linger.

YOUNGER SISTER: I'll stay. I'm not leaving.

M: If you still want me in daylight. I should have stayed with you from the beginning.

YOUNGER SISTER: You still can.

M: But I'm broken. You're getting a tattered shadow.

(The wolves again, closer this time.)

YOUNGER SISTER: The wolves. Please come.

M: It doesn't make any difference.

YOUNGER SISTER: There they are.

(Some way off: the DOG, with a torn-off leash around his neck.)

DOG: I smelled you. Good, eh?

YOUNGER SISTER: Go away.

DOG: I smelled you from such all that distance.

M: And now?

DOG: You smell good. I like it.

YOUNGER SISTER: He means your blood, because you're hurt.

M: I don't care what he means, that's not a wolf, it's a dog.

DOG: I live with the wolves now, my master wanted to eat me, he'd already put the noose round my neck to strangle me.

YOUNGER SISTER: A dog leash, that's normal.

DOG: But I tore the leash and ran away. He whistled but I pretended not to hear. My legs were tingling, they wanted to run back to him, but my nose forced them in the other direction, into the steppe, towards the wolves.

M: Your master died tonight.

DOG: I know, I can smell it on you. I like the way you smell although I'm with the wolves now. Two people, I had to come because I'm hungry, none of the wolves managed to smell it across such a great distance. Just me. Good, eh?

YOUNGER SISTER: And now you'll show them the way so they can come and eat us.

DOG: You belong to us, the smell between your legs is nice too, I know you'll slap my nose if I get too close, but it really turns me on, are you coming?

M: To see the wolves?

YOUNGER SISTER: If you want to eat us you'll have to come to us.

DOG: *(To M.)* We race across the steppe under the moon, and the light makes us look silver, we're strong because there are so many of us, a pack, one of them is running in front of me and there's one on each side, and even more behind me, I can feel their strides in the ground, and my stride is the same as theirs because they're my brothers, and I can lose myself in this common stride, and we keep up the pace and no one says sit, stay or fetch, and sometimes we all stop at once because someone's held their nose in the wind at the front, and we find a lost goat dried-out and half dead in the sand, and then we tilt our heads back and howl a song, and in the distance the other wolves answer with a similar song, there are so many of us, loads, we rule the entire steppe. You have to run with us. You can't stay with people who want to put you on a leash.

M: Maybe he's right.

YOUNGER SISTER: But you're not a wolf.

DOG: *(To M.)* It doesn't take long when the others are running alongside you and the moon flows through you.

YOUNGER SISTER: *(To M.)* Don't trust him, they'll eat you.

DOG: And one day I'll return to the city, the leader of the pack, then there's a huge hunt and we'll pull out everything that's still alive and have a huge meal with bare bones in the moonlight, don't you want to join us?

YOUNGER SISTER: He's not hungry, he had mussels.

M: *(To the DOG.)* In August, I know.

DOG: *(To M.)* You're already one of us. You've already started, I can smell it on your hands, you've already been hunting and eaten without us.

M: Maybe if we go with him people will leave us alone.

YOUNGER SISTER: The people aren't here yet, we just have to make it till morning.

M: You said they'd risen up all over the city to hunt me.

DOG: They daren't come to the wolves.

YOUNGER SISTER: I daren't go to the wolves either.

DOG: So you'll stay here.

M: You said droves of them are chasing through the streets and over the parched fields of the steppe because they can smell me.

YOUNGER SISTER: Don't you understand? They're going to eat you.

M: The people.

YOUNGER SISTER: No, the wolves.

M: I'd rather the wolves than the people.

DOG: Are you coming?

(M starts to move.)

YOUNGER SISTER: So you're leaving me here.

DOG: We're not leaving anything. Those that don't run with us are prey.

(To M.) Smell that?

M: What?

DOG: That's fear.

YOUNGER SISTER: *(To the DOG.)* Stay there.

DOG: I can smell it. The smell makes my blood boil.

YOUNGER SISTER: Sit.

DOG: Sit is over, it's broken, it doesn't mean anything now.

YOUNGER SISTER: Stay.

DOG: I'm not staying either, I'm a wolf. I'm hungry. I can smell your blood. I can smell your fear. You turn me on.

YOUNGER SISTER: *(To M.)* Why are you just standing there?

DOG: *(To the YOUNGER SISTER.)* You got too close with your smell.

(To M.) Come on brother, let's get her.

(The DOG and M attack the YOUNGER SISTER. When they separate a few moments later, we see that M attacked the DOG, not the YOUNGER SISTER, and has stabbed him.)

M: That's my blood you can smell, and my fear.

DOG: My brothers will come. They'll smell that you've eaten me.

M: I'm not going to eat you.

DOG: The whole pack is going to sink their teeth into you, wolf after wolf, and when you run away and flail your arms to try and shake them off you'll look like an animal in the silver light, an animal with a hundred furry arms dancing in the moonlight before you collapse, and then they'll tilt their heads back and howl. I was good, I smelled you.

(He stops moving. The wolves howl. Nothing.)

YOUNGER SISTER: We need to go.

M: Where to?

YOUNGER SISTER: There's a country road behind the steppe. My parents had a holiday cottage there, when I was a child I could slip through a hatch in the basement, maybe I still can. I'm still as thin as I was then.

M: Because you don't eat. Aren't you hungry?

YOUNGER SISTER: We'd be safe there. You can lie on the bed and rest and when the sun is high in the sky we'll go outside and fetch water from the cistern, there are brambles behind the house, my father planted potatoes, maybe we can still find some in the earth by the fence.

M: Yes, that would be nice.

YOUNGER SISTER: We'll sit at the table and look forward to the following day.

M: But the night's in between.

YOUNGER SISTER: I'm not afraid of that. There's two of us.

M: Exactly.

YOUNGER SISTER: I'll hold your hand when you fall asleep.

M: Nice. Why would you do that for me?

YOUNGER SISTER: Do you really need to know?

M: Because of the way you look at me.

YOUNGER SISTER: How?

M: Concerned, maybe.

YOUNGER SISTER: Yes. Because I care about how you feel.

M: Yes, as if you're interested in me.

YOUNGER SISTER: Yes. Because I want us to stay together.

M: Yes, as if you're interested in me.

YOUNGER SISTER: I am.

M: As if you're interested in my throat.

YOUNGER SISTER: What?

M: You're looking at my throat, between my Adam's apple and my neck.

YOUNGER SISTER: Am I?

M: Yes. As if you're interested in that particular part of me.

YOUNGER SISTER: I'm not sure that's true.

M: As if you're hungry.

YOUNGER SISTER: Hungry?

M: Are you hungry?

YOUNGER SISTER: Let's keep walking.

M: I need to know if you're hungry.

YOUNGER SISTER: The wolves are going to come.

M: I know you're hungry.

(Nothing.)

YOUNGER SISTER: Do you have to stab me now?

M: Is that why you looked at me like that?

YOUNGER SISTER: I can't help it.

M: No?

YOUNGER SISTER: But I would never –

M: Of course not.

YOUNGER SISTER: I don't want to eat you.

M: But you can't help it.

YOUNGER SISTER: But up to now I've been able to. Your flesh is pink, there, at your throat.

M: Please look somewhere else.

YOUNGER SISTER: If you think it's the only way I won't fight.

M: What?

YOUNGER SISTER: I don't want things to go that far. Stab me now, before it's too late.

M: Go how far?

YOUNGER SISTER: That the hunger drives me crazy and I have to attack you.

M: Is that going to happen?

YOUNGER SISTER: I don't know.

M: If you think it's the only way I won't fight.

YOUNGER SISTER: What?

M: I don't want this anymore.

YOUNGER SISTER: But at some point you'll probably have to.

M: There have been so many already. And each time I get heavier.

YOUNGER SISTER: You've almost made it, it's only me now.

M: I'd rather give you a miss.

YOUNGER SISTER: Why?

M: If you want to eat me, go ahead.

YOUNGER SISTER: Why do you say that?

M: If you're hungry.

(She approaches him tentatively. It could turn into a bite but turns into a kiss.)

YOUNGER SISTER: It'll be light soon.

M: Let's wait till it gets light.

(They sit down. Between them, on the ground, is the knife. They look at each other. Nothing.)

YOUNGER SISTER: Are you scared?

M: No.

YOUNGER SISTER: Then why are you looking at me like that?

(He looks away. She keeps looking at him. Nothing.)

M: *(Without looking at her.)* Are you scared?

(She looks away. Gradually it gets light. We hear the wolves howling.)

The End

ELDORADO

Eldorado was first performed at the Schaubühne am Lehniner Platz on 11 December 2004, directed by Thomas Ostermeier.

It was first performed in the UK at the Arcola Theatre, London, on 26 March 2014, directed by Simon Dormandy.

Characters

ASCHENBRENNER
Anton's boss

THEKLA
mid-thirties

ANTON
mid-thirties

GRETA
Thekla's mother

OSKAR
mid-thirties

MANUELA
early twenties

1.

ASCHENBRENNER: In the distance, beyond the forest, helicopters have ascended, a dark swarm in an echelon formation, they pull up over the city with a shredding drone, teeter over the gasworks, then tilt towards the train station. Shortly afterwards, when the first shots have smashed through the glass roof and sliced open a train standing on the tracks, a black squadron of tactical aircraft cuts through the red sky. It's the beginning of the first wave of attacks. Three months later, we're faced with an extraordinary challenge. Seen from above, the contours of the area resemble a decapitated head. The northernmost point is the veterans' cemetery, where the toppled gravestones appear white against the wreckage of the surrounding area. The smell of burned tropical woods drifts across from the western border: the botanical gardens have burned down to the edge of the riverbank, the orchid house has burst from the heat, and the animals have followed their instincts and abandoned the adjoining zoo. Now they're roaming through the ruins of the government quarter, drinking from the fountains someone has forgotten about, but that's beside the point. By the southern border lies the sports stadium, which has to be conserved in its present condition. When the wind is right, you can hear the refugees' voices ringing out from the oval concrete. If you continue east past the torched wrecks by the side of the motorway, you get to the cadet schools and refineries that were the outermost targets. In the autumn, a murder of crows circles here. Over a total area spanning more than eighty square kilometres, our company is today able to offer you an investment opportunity with unique historic prospects. Here history has entrusted the investor with a piece of the world. A piece of the world that looks almost virginal in the glow of the morning sun.

2.

THEKLA: I just need the garden and a room for the piano.

ANTON: The stairs are for the nursery.

THEKLA: That's news to me.

ANTON: If the tree bothers you we'll get rid of it.

THEKLA: We'll put the barbecue on the lawn and burn sausages, and when it gets loud on the other side of the fence we'll throw water bombs. We need a pergola as well.

ANTON: *(Friendly.)* Yes.

THEKLA: No reason to get into a bad mood.

ANTON: I'm not. Pergola.

THEKLA: Wild wine. And a pond with fish in it. We'll make love on a swinging bench. A birch tree.

ANTON: *(Friendly.)* I don't know when I'll have time.

THEKLA: No need to shout.

ANTON: I'm not shouting, I'm thinking.

THEKLA: We're just getting started. You should be pleased I'm not sitting on the stairs to the nursery, crying.

ANTON: I am. You'll get your birch tree.

THEKLA: It's going to be lovely. A bird just landed in the tree.

3.

ANTON: Please don't destroy me.

ASCHENBRENNER: You've destroyed yourself. You've massacred yourself. Does it bother you when I stare at you like this? You don't have to be polite anymore.

ANTON: If you tell the legal department, you'll blow up my foundations.

ASCHENBRENNER: I don't find this embarrassing. From a professional point of view, you leave me cold. I've sent lots of people to their social deaths without flinching. The only interesting thing about you is my personal failure. That's why I feel sorry for you.

ANTON: I shocked myself.

ASCHENBRENNER: Does the South Pacific mean anything to you? When I was there, a lantern-eye fish swam past my diving mask. His eyes glow when the sea gets dark, so the small fish, attracted by the iridescence down below, venture in front of his mouth, and then he closes his teeth around his prey. You're one of those lantern-eye fish. Your face is a trap, lethal seriousness shines from your eyes, and we wander in drunk with naive trust, not noticing your stupid mouth that shows you're stupid, after all the lantern-eye fish is related to the slimehead – you've got those eyes so we don't notice when your stupid mouth snaps shut. I bet you spend your whole time staring into your serious eyes in the mirror and hypnotising your brain into stupidity. Now you're snapping.

ANTON: I have a wife. We're about to buy –

ASCHENBRENNER: Wrong. You're not a cleaning lady. Say something else.

ANTON: I can't think of anything.

ASCHENBRENNER: Then improvise – isn't that your specialty? Fake yourself.

(Nothing.)

Pathetic. I don't mind you underestimating me, your entire disposition is wrong; your brain is probably a prosthetic. Here. Sign my name under your dismissal.

ANTON: Where? I don't understand, this is where –

ASCHENBRENNER: I want to see you do it.

ANTON: No no, you're the one who's supposed to –. I see. You mean, funny, your signature – I'm not that quick, humour-wise.

ASCHENBRENNER: I don't have a sense of humour. My signature. So there's a point to you having practised for the last couple of months. Squeamish? As if it was your first time.

ANTON: I don't know on what level you want to ruin me now.

ASCHENBRENNER: There aren't many left.

(ANTON tries to laugh. It's a pathetic attempt.)

ASCHENBRENNER: *(Shouts at him.)* My signature, slimehead!

(ANTON signs.)

ASCHENBRENNER: So you made yourself useful after all. So this is me. You had talent.

4.

GRETA: You're beautiful when you've got that stupid look on your face.

OSKAR: I'm looking straight ahead.

ANTON: They tore the palace apart themselves a while ago, they dismantled it from top to bottom, stone by stone, they numbered and filed everything, every column, every statue, all of it.

OSKAR: And then they stored the building in the wine cellar. You're drunk.

ANTON: Not in the cellar. An underground system of bunkers and corridors. Everything was flooded with water, but the basic structure has survived, and they've got the plans, so they can rebuild it just the way it was.

OSKAR: What's this?

ANTON: The ground surrounding the refineries is contaminated, so I'd advise against it. It could take decades.

OSKAR: But it's green.

GRETA: Give me your mouth.

OSKAR: I'm talking.

GRETA: You're chattering. Anton is in politics.

ANTON: I'm in real estate.

GRETA: I want to drink wine and fall into a sexual trance so I can forget this unbearable evening.

OSKAR: I thought it was nice.

GRETA: She's a failure. Where is she, anyway? I hope she's crying.

ANTON: Freshening up.

GRETA: She's taking too much of that stuff, tell her that.

(To OSKAR.) And you have no sensuality.

OSKAR: I'm discussing financial prospects. I can't put my tongue in your ear at the same time.

GRETA: I don't mind that you're after my money; I know how to use my assets. My legs are still firm.

OSKAR: And this?

ANTON: That's the street where they hanged people from the lamp posts in the transition period. We can't touch the government quarter. I've reserved an appropriate block for you and Oskar.

GRETA: 'You and Oskar.' I just keep him for fun.

OSKAR: That's something.

ANTON: I'm not going to talk you into anything. You're small fry by comparison.

(We can hear a piano.)

OSKAR: What's happening?

GRETA: She might as well have put her arse on the keyboard. I feel low.

ANTON: This is what she does when she's messed up a concert. It'll go on all night.

OSKAR: I don't think she messed up. I couldn't do that. All those keys.

GRETA: You're no yardstick. She's hitting the keys, it's like she's playing with hooves, it's an ambush, we're finished.

ANTON: Those are moments of infinite solitude, she's going to punish herself till she gets sore.

GRETA: We're the ones who are being punished, I wonder why, I wore a stole to a community centre and I didn't look at her hands, I've nothing to reproach myself with. Go and put her out of her misery, give her some drops or slam the lid.

ANTON: Sometimes she cries herself to sleep with her face on her fingers.

(He leaves.)

GRETA: Tell her to be quiet or I'll come and help her practise.

OSKAR: We shouldn't dilly-dally for too long or we'll lose out on the profit.

GRETA: 'The noble woods are burgeoning with flowers and leaves.'

OSKAR: No.

GRETA: 'Where is the lover I knew?
He has ridden off!
Who will love me?'

OSKAR: Stop it, it's embarrassing.

GRETA: This is an opportunity to show some passion.

OSKAR: I'm supposed to throw you on the cushions now that he's about to walk in with Thekla.

GRETA: I don't like the way you say her name. Get over it. You slid down the stairs on mattresses with her when you were children, but now she's grown up and she wants to play grown-up mattress games. But when she looks at you that doesn't even enter her head. You look like a soft toy.

(The piano-playing stops.)

OSKAR: I know where I stand and I'm not going to complain. Stop it.

GRETA: Don't panic, I'm just pulling the stocking over my knee.

OSKAR: I can smell you from here.

GRETA: Then loosen your tie.

OSKAR: What gland is that smell coming from?

GRETA: See if you can find it.

(OSKAR starts to grope her.)

OSKAR: You're a gorgeous slut.

GRETA: You're not going to score by being vulgar.

(THEKLA enters with ANTON.)

THEKLA: Anton says you've missed me. Doesn't look like it, Anton. What are they doing?

GRETA: Oskar is helping me close my *collier*, which is undone.

THEKLA: I thought he was strangling you.

OSKAR: On the contrary.

THEKLA: Is there a contrary? I know I've got an obscene mother, but when you stroke her she's really sweet.

GRETA: How many did you take?

THEKLA: There's some ice left in the freezer if you want to cool your synapses.

GRETA: Anton, you need to lock that stuff up, look at her.

THEKLA: If you want I can act like a madwoman and throw cactuses around.

GRETA: Maybe if you took the pills before the concert you'd be a bit more gentle with the instrument. Your left hand is a disaster, and I mean well.

(THEKLA leaves.)

Your husband says we're small fry.

OSKAR: Where is she going?

ANTON: I said by comparison. We're talking billions here. Multiple digits.

OSKAR: The whole complex is too expensive. We'll go for the west wing, and then we've got sixty percent.

(We hear the piano again.)

ANTON: I'll have to check. They're trying to keep the complex together.

GRETA: We'll take the whole thing.

OSKAR: Greta, we're being sensible here.

GRETA: So am I. The whole thing.

OSKAR: We haven't got that much.

GRETA: You don't, that's for sure. We'll take the whole complex, thirty living units and five retail. Don't give me that fishy look, it's not your money. I want a memorial, terraced all the way down to the lower floors, a central life cell with a fountain and an artist's mobile with amplitudes that span several metres in a glass-roof atrium. That's the future down there, it's for the people whose heads they shot through, where there were rapes and ugly details and thousands in tents at the airport. We're going in there with our money and we're paving the way for humanity. It's a positive thing.

OSKAR: I seriously think that you should talk to someone before you do something of this magnitude.

GRETA: My husband's dead. I'm talking to Anton, who is an expert and who has seen their distress.

(There's a thud, and the piano-playing stops.)

Dreadful, the way she's hitting the keys.

OSKAR: I think you should consult an independent voice.

ANTON: You can ask whoever you want –

GRETA: He's talking about himself. I'm supposed to let him run the company.

OSKAR: Isn't that why you need me?

GRETA: Everyone knows why I need you.

OSKAR: I won't be reduced to that.

GRETA: You've calculated my prospects. I'm the one who has sole signatory power, you'll have to live with that.

OSKAR: You're only doing this because you want to humiliate me.

GRETA: It's not worth the effort.

(THEKLA returns.)

THEKLA: Isn't it time you went to bed?

GRETA: I need your husband in private for a moment.

THEKLA: I don't like it when you make unsavoury remarks. Your mouth is dripping.

GRETA: Anton, tell her to go dig in the garden or something, I want to get through this today.

THEKLA: I hereby announce the end of my career as a solo pianist.

GRETA: Nonsense, go to bed. It wasn't much of a career.

THEKLA: I'm not putting my fingers into that mouth with white elephant teeth anymore. After many long, futile years I'm drawing the line. So that's it. Now you can get the contracts ready.

GRETA: No doubt about it: you're having a crisis.

THEKLA: I tried to break my hand with the piano lid, but I haven't got the guts. Just a swelling.

ANTON: Your precious hands.

THEKLA: Don't want them anymore.

GRETA: You mustn't destroy your hands, they're not yours, they belong to the world, and to art.

THEKLA: The music falls apart in my ears. I can't hear the tune anymore. Just noise. I play the typewriter with so and so many hits per minute. I panic and shoot at everything that moves, it's an unprecedented decline.

OSKAR: *(Takes her hand.)* Squashed and bruised. In terms of organs it's not serious.

THEKLA: You don't know anything. The concert halls are full of assassins these days, if you sit in the balcony you can watch dead people falling into the stalls and then someone turns round and says, 'shush'. They used to shoot them from the box, from behind the curtain, but now they're really laid back, they put the machine gun in the dress circle, in full view of everyone, politely let the audience go past and then shoot when the orchestra starts to play, they shoot the ones they don't need in the rows or on stage, and the smoke rises up into the extinguished chandelier. I've lost the music in all this carnage.

GRETA: Highly strung gestures. There are no boxes or chandeliers where you play. Community centres. You were bad, that's all. We'll start early tomorrow.

ANTON: Leave her alone.

(To THEKLA.) I'll put you to bed. I'll sing in your ear and hold my hand over your eyes.

THEKLA: Today I thought the hall was sinking. It tipped over sideways and went under, and everyone in the stalls stayed in their seats when the water rose, and in the end there were toupees floating on the waves and in the balconies the audience applauded the sinking ship. And I sat behind my instrument, my tense fingers sending Morse code to deaf ears. Save our souls. I quit.

ANTON: Sleep. Tomorrow you'll see the world with different eyes.

(He exits with her.)

GRETA: *(To OSKAR.)* You're really beautiful when you've got that stupid look on your face. So it's a crisis. Picturesque.

5.

MANUELA: Are you listening?

THEKLA: Every note. Keep playing.

MANUELA: You're looking out the window the whole time.

THEKLA: I should cut some of the branches, the cherries will fall through the open window and onto the carpet.

MANUELA: I feel as if I'm bothering you.

THEKLA: Last night you were crying.

MANUELA: I'm sorry. I thought you couldn't see that from the stage.

THEKLA: At least there was one person in that dumb crowd who was touched. You're talented.

MANUELA: Yes.

THEKLA: Why don't you want to enter competitions? At your age I – how old are you?

MANUELA: It damages one's artistic development.

THEKLA: Aha?

MANUELA: It squanders one's talent ahead of time.

THEKLA: Aha.

MANUELA: Music is not a sport.

THEKLA: Cherry branches look nice in a vase as well.

MANUELA: Ten years from now I don't want to be used up with no hinterland.

THEKLA: But he shouldn't put the flowers on the piano. It feels like we're sitting round a decorated coffin.

MANUELA: I've been wanting to tell you. Can you hear me?

THEKLA: Every note.

MANUELA: I need bigger challenges. The pieces you've been giving me – I can tell from every note what I'm meant to learn. But now it has to be about the music.

THEKLA: It always is.

MANUELA: Great music.

THEKLA: I would have waited another six months.

MANUELA: I'm stagnating.

THEKLA: We can do the Schumann concerto. I don't mind artistic impatience. You have to find your own way.

MANUELA: What I'm trying to say is: I'm not going to do it with you.

THEKLA: And who are you going to do it with?

MANUELA: I don't think there's anything left that I can learn from you.

THEKLA: That depends on you.

MANUELA: What I mean is: I don't think there's anything left that you can teach me.

THEKLA: Aha.

MANUELA: It's not personal. I like you, and I like your garden as well.

THEKLA: I played the Schumann concerto at your age, I won the Liszt Prize.

MANUELA: I know.

THEKLA: I know. It's a long time ago.

MANUELA: You were good for me for a long time, but now –

THEKLA: I'm no longer good enough.

MANUELA: I didn't say that.

THEKLA: And who's better?

MANUELA: I wouldn't like to say.

THEKLA: Christian.

MANUELA: I'd rather not say anything.

THEKLA: Christian is going to mess you up, he's got no ear for you.

MANUELA: I have to find my own way. This isn't easy for me either.

THEKLA: I didn't say this was difficult for me, I've got other students, I'm just sorry about your talent.

MANUELA: It would be nice if we could do this without arguing.

THEKLA: All of a sudden you're a stranger. Only yesterday you sat there and cried.

MANUELA: With pity. It was such a pointless struggle in the community centre. I realised the full extent of your tragedy.

THEKLA: Yes. It really is for the best.

MANUELA: I used to admire you a great deal.

THEKLA: As if I was dead already. You'll have to completely change your technique.

MANUELA: Precisely. That's what it's all about. I still owe you money.

THEKLA: You can call me Thekla if you want. I don't need any authority now.

MANUELA: Thanks. I'd rather not.

6.

ANTON: I couldn't get an appointment.

ASCHENBRENNER: That was deliberate. I've no idea what you want.

ANTON: I want my job back.

ASCHENBRENNER: It's not your job and you have no rights. I'll have you thrown out the window.

ANTON: This briefcase is going to help me keep my job.

ASCHENBRENNER: You're standing on a trap door. When I push this button it opens and you slide through the scrap chute down into the canteen waste. Was that clear enough?

ANTON: I'll keep working for you even if you throw me into the potato peels. No one can replace me.

ASCHENBRENNER: Cheeky. You haven't been able to cope with all your free time. You've got rings under your eyes. You need airing. Dissolve an aspirin.

ANTON: I've got the finished contract in this briefcase. A whole complex, with signatures and witnessed, the first instalments are already in my account.

ASCHENBRENNER: You're delirious with fever. I'm going to call your wife and then you're going home to bed with a hot water bottle. You're shattered.

ANTON: My wife isn't stable, she'll jump out the window into the garden with worry. It's one of the complexes by the northern exit road, between the market halls and the bus terminus. We're developing a completely new part of the city.

ASCHENBRENNER: What's the world coming to? Let me take your hand. The city down there is crowded with people. Have you thought about where they're going to detonate the first bombs? There are drawers somewhere in this world that hold plans for the attack, they've even calculated the body count. Have you thought about where you want to be on that morning? Do you want to die in the street, in an exploding car, do you want your head to be crushed by debris from a collapsing house, or do you want a clean shot in the body when you step out of the bakery? Someone else is shaping this city, not you. Go and live in the country. Put turnips in the ground and build a chicken coop. I mean well. This is no place for you. You tried it for a while with my name, but I'm not giving you my chair. It's you or me. And of course it's me, not you.

ANTON: You don't know what you're doing, you're an amateur. You'll go to the dogs.

ASCHENBRENNER: Bundle yourself and your briefcase down into the city. You may take the lift.

7.

THEKLA: I'm going to dig up the garden and plant forsythias.

GRETA: Aha.

THEKLA: You look as if there's a collision in your brain.

GRETA: You don't want to take on new students?

THEKLA: I want to pull up weeds.

GRETA: Highly strung.

OSKAR: And in the winter?

THEKLA: Don't know. Maybe I'll grow cactuses with UV light or fly to the equator.

GRETA: I think that's completely deranged.

OSKAR: You're being too radical.

GRETA: She's pumped litres of sweat into her existence, and now she's voluntarily diving back into mediocrity.

THEKLA: I never left it.

GRETA: One snotty-nosed pupil has a tantrum and you sink and deliberately become unfit for society.

THEKLA: Anton earns enough money to feed three families.

GRETA: I know how successful Anton is, that's not the point. *(To ANTON.)* I spent years sitting on the stool behind her waiting for her crooked fingers to reach the octaves.

THEKLA: I want to watch plants grow.

GRETA: But the music.

THEKLA: Doesn't need me. I'll lock the room and bury the key under the compost heap.

OSKAR: None of this is my business, but –

GRETA: *(Interrupting OSKAR.)* Exactly.

(To THEKLA.) You need therapy.

(To ANTON.) She needs therapy, Anton, common sense won't get us anywhere with her.

THEKLA: I feel better than I've done in years.

GRETA: And that's not normal.

OSKAR: What I was trying to say was: what's so bad about her having a break?

THEKLA: I'm not having a break.

GRETA: She's not having a break. Because if she is she can cross me out of her address book, I don't associate with housewives and gardeners, I won't let her ruin her life just because she thinks it'll hurt me. You're hurting yourself, you stupid cow, you can throw away your career when you have one, when it would cause a scandal and a public outcry, but you're just drowning.

OSKAR: If it's a creative –

GRETA: Shut up. Creative.
(To THEKLA.) I'll give you an address. He can fix this.

(Storms off.)

OSKAR: I'm sorry –

ANTON: Sure, no problem.

(OSKAR exits.)

THEKLA: Don't pull that face, Anton. My personality isn't going to change because of this, and if it does it can only get better.

ANTON: I don't mind your personality.

THEKLA: It's nice that you're being supportive.

ANTON: Thekla, there's something I need to bring up. What you said about me having enough money to feed three families –

THEKLA: I know what you're trying to say: we're not a family yet.

ANTON: No, what I'm trying to say is – our life has to change. Everything will have to be different in the future.

THEKLA: Exactly. It's already different.

ANTON: What?

THEKLA: I'm not just doing this because I'm not talented enough. I went to the doctor's and I'm pregnant.

ANTON: Oh.

THEKLA: We're having a baby.

ANTON: All of a sudden.

THEKLA: Yes. For our nursery.

ANTON: I don't know what to say. I'm shocked.

THEKLA: It's natural that you're deeply moved, you've always wanted this. In the summer we'll blow up a paddling pool in the garden and go strawberry picking in the plantations out of town, in the winter we'll have a fir tree with candles and we'll make biscuits and watch our daughter grow. And the bigger she gets the smaller we'll get until we disappear and everything belongs to her. That's what it's all about, that's the whole purpose, and soon we'll be a part of all that.

ANTON: You've no idea what this means to me.

THEKLA: I love you, Anton. Even more now.

ANTON: I love you too.

THEKLA: What was it you were going to say?

ANTON: Nothing, nothing at all. There's no point now. Nothing.

THEKLA: Right.

8.

OSKAR: Are you watching the lobsters behind the glass?

ANTON: I didn't recognise you with the shopping bags.

OSKAR: Didn't you just come out of that hotel?

ANTON: Me? No. Everything all right?

OSKAR: Couple of errands. Originally I wanted them to kill a pike, but the catfish had such long barbels that he had to die instead.

ANTON: The catfish.

OSKAR: I can't get over it.

ANTON: It's just a fish, it doesn't even have warm blood.

OSKAR: I mean, I was sure you just came out of that hotel –

ANTON: Must have been someone else. I look like everyone else.

OSKAR: And you stare into fishmongers' shops in the middle of the day? You must be waiting for someone.

ANTON: Me? No. For whom?

OSKAR: You're just watching the lobsters?

ANTON: There's no law against that, is there?

OSKAR: No. I thought you'd be at work, I didn't expect to see you here.

ANTON: Work, yes, what time is it?

OSKAR: Half past twelve.

ANTON: Right, my lunch break. I often take advantage of my lunch break.

OSKAR: To watch lobsters.

ANTON: Exactly. They've got rubber bands round their claws, they're waiting for someone to pull them out of the cool water and drop them into a pot filled with boiling broth. It makes me philosophical. In my lunch break. It's relaxing.

OSKAR: Aha.

ANTON: Relieves aggression for the day.

OSKAR: Between you and Aschenbrenner?

ANTON: No no. Personal tension, I keep the office clean.

OSKAR: You must all be in a state of emotional emergency with the region still on fire, the insurgencies, you're very much identified with the project.

ANTON: It's all stable.

OSKAR: I can understand that you seek refuge in these slow, elegant animals.

ANTON: The project is secure, those are the final skirmishes, and with something this big it doesn't matter if a rebel from the north blows himself up somewhere.

OSKAR: So it's not private.

ANTON: What?

OSKAR: I mean you're not looking at moss-covered seafood because there's private tension between Thekla and you?

(ANTON laughs.)

ANTON: You see, I didn't even get that. Not at all. And you're all right? What are you up to?

OSKAR: Yes, a couple of errands. The sad catfish. Dry Riesling. Greta is having a dinner party and I'm cooking, you know what it's like.

ANTON: Not really. Well. I should get going.

OSKAR: Don't you work in that tower at the other end of town anymore?

ANTON: The tower. No, not anymore, we've got a branch office now, I'm now running the branch office.

OSKAR: A promotion.

ANTON: Quasi.

OSKAR: That's nice, Thekla must be proud of you.

ANTON: Yes, very. Very proud, Thekla.

OSKAR: And you really didn't come out of that hotel?

ANTON: I think I'd know. I should go, I've got three men waiting for me.

9.

THEKLA: You look terrible.

ANTON: My head's buzzing. I slept wrong last night.

THEKLA: All discoloured round your eyes.

ANTON: Mislaid my head.

THEKLA: You whistled in bed.

ANTON: Whistled?

THEKLA: Like this.

(She whistles.)

You shouldn't whistle where you sleep, it's rude.

ANTON: It was a rough night, I can't remember.

THEKLA: Makes me want to cry when you're like this. Visiting from the other side.

ANTON: But I'm nice.

THEKLA: You're terrified. Your work has gnawed at your bones. He's whipping you into self-abandonment.

ANTON: Who's whipping me?

THEKLA: Aschenbrenner. If you keep working this hard there'll be nothing left of you. You used to take an interest in fish.

ANTON: I've had lots of time off since the last deal.

THEKLA: How am I supposed to know, you don't tell me anything. I can go for days without knowing what you're up to.

ANTON: I often don't know myself.

THEKLA: I read that there are riots in the government quarter.

ANTON: Thekla, I want to make a deal with you.

THEKLA: What? What does that look mean?

ANTON: Once I've stepped through this door I don't want to hear or say anything about my job. A large part of my brain is always at the office anyway. I'm going gaga. I think in terms of grid squares and field sections. I can't even look at a house without thinking about where they're going to attach the charge to blow it up. In our house the load-bearing wall goes through the bedroom. I want this place to be clear of all that. You're here. I want to look at your beautiful face and not see ruins. I want a safe place. Can you understand that?

THEKLA: Yes. You're pushing me out of your life.

ANTON: No, I want you to pull me into your life, I want to stand under the rhododendron with you and not hear Aschenbrenner's bulldozer in my head, I want to stay sane.

THEKLA: Yes.

ANTON: Can you do that for me?

THEKLA: I'll think about it.

ANTON: I've got three men waiting for me, I have to go.

THEKLA: You haven't eaten anything.

ANTON: I'll have the coffee.

THEKLA: Drink slowly, I'll get your coat.

(She leaves.)

You were whistling a march as if it was the Last Judgement. It's ruined my day.

ANTON: As far as I'm concerned it might as well be night, I wouldn't mind giving the dance a miss today. Let's go to bed.

(Nothing.)

I said I'm fine, we can skip the day, that's fine with me, and go to bed – oh never mind.

(Nothing.)

Did the hallway swallow you up?

THEKLA: There's an odd substance stuck to the carpet.

ANTON: What?

THEKLA: There's something smeared across the hallway.

ANTON: I have to go.

THEKLA: I don't know what it is.

(ANTON goes to THEKLA.)

ANTON: Dirt. It's dirt.

THEKLA: In the shape of a trail.

ANTON: I shouldn't have stood up so quickly.

THEKLA: Footprints.

ANTON: I'm going to black out.

THEKLA: From a foot. Don't step in it.

ANTON: My head's buzzing, I need to sit down.

THEKLA: From a shoe. From there to there and into our home.

ANTON: Okay. Let's get rid of the dirt.

THEKLA: Is it dirt? Soil.

ANTON: Whatever it is, I don't want it in the hallway.

THEKLA: Dried and stuck to the fibre structure. Who would bring something like that in here? A sole profile.

ANTON: I think we should –

THEKLA: And here.

ANTON: Should just get rid of it.

THEKLA: Little lumps.

ANTON: Someone is going to end up stepping – and bring it into the house. The dirt.

THEKLA: With fir needles in it. Look, two needles.

ANTON: My head's buzzing. My coffee.

THEKLA: Fir needles. Pines.

ANTON: I'll phone them and they can lather the whole carpet while they're at it.

THEKLA: But we don't even know –

ANTON: Someone walked from there to there. And dropped dirt. I can't get my head round it.

THEKLA: But who, we don't know –

ANTON: I'll phone them.

THEKLA: But –

ANTON: You're not normally like this.

THEKLA: I just want to know, these needles –

ANTON: I'll take care of it. My coffee, I have to go. I've got three men waiting for me.

THEKLA: Maybe the person is still in our house.

10.

OSKAR: Anton, we're shocked.

ANTON: It's actually good news.

OSKAR: We bought a concept without old rubble. New rubble if you like, but not a collapsed heritage site.

ANTON: The people that lived there two thousand years ago weren't to know that you want to dig an underground car park there. The tomb is a fact.

OSKAR: But we don't want it. Why don't they just blow away the foundations like the rest of the city?

ANTON: There are enamelled bowls in the ground, armed mummies and even a horse skeleton with gold jewellery.

OSKAR: Cadavers. Great.

GRETA: There are plenty of those anyway.

OSKAR: But none that are two thousand years old –

ANTON: That first night people broke in and ransacked the place.

OSKAR: So then everything's gone and the excavators can start.

ANTON: Now there's a massive military presence securing it. The tomb is a cultural sensation.

OSKAR: A pile of shrivelled corpses.

GRETA: When can we start building?

ANTON: We have to wait till they've dug everything up and shipped it. The planning of the building is more complicated now, they want us to integrate the prehistoric traits. Our proposal is to not plaster the brickwork and to put a glass floor over the vault. The property will be an architectural masterpiece of an international standard.

OSKAR: And twice as expensive.

ANTON: According to our calculations, not quite.

OSKAR: *(To GRETA.)* I told you: the city is dead and dead things stink.

(To ANTON.) You've sold us a rotten fish and now you say the rot is special and costs extra and try to sell it to us a second time – at an inflated price. I'm not getting personal here, but that's a scam.

(To GRETA.) We'll be throwing more and more money into that hole every year, I warned you from the start, and that's why we're going to sell this money pit as quickly as possible.

ANTON: You can do that, of course. The tourist industry pays triple dollar for property on historic ground. A restaurant with a view of the catacombs –

OSKAR: Who wants to look at that when they're eating?

GRETA: *(To OSKAR.)* Stupid man, you're getting worked up.

OSKAR: Isn't it true?

GRETA: *(To ANTON.)* Send me the new calculation. I'll see the boy home.

OSKAR: I'm going to bite the carpet.

GRETA: If possible with a ground plan for the restaurant.

ANTON: Of course.

GRETA: *(To OSKAR.)* You're beautiful when you've got that stupid look on your face.

OSKAR: You're only doing this to humiliate me.

GRETA: I can afford it.

11.

(MANUELA is playing the piano, ANTON is listening. THEKLA comes home and switches on the light.)

THEKLA: Who's playing?

MANUELA: Sorry.

ANTON: I was worried.

THEKLA: I was at the doctor's. Why are you sitting in the dark?

ANTON: We were waiting for you.

THEKLA: With no light.

MANUELA: My fault. When I got here the sun was still in the room like when I used to have my lesson.

ANTON: I was worried, she played the piano.

THEKLA: I went to see the doctor.

ANTON: Right.

THEKLA: Why did you open the room?

MANUELA: I missed the view of the cherries. I'm not happy, I want to come back.

THEKLA: Because you miss the cherry tree?

MANUELA: I'm losing everything.

THEKLA: That's normal.

(To ANTON.) And you just sit there and listen to her hitting the instrument? It's irritating.

ANTON: That was Schumann. You used to play it.

THEKLA: I know who composed it.

ANTON: Of course.

THEKLA: And?

ANTON: And what?

THEKLA: Does she play well?

ANTON: I can't tell.

THEKLA: Of course her playing is divine. Now there are lots of moths.

MANUELA: Because you switched the light on.

THEKLA: What was I supposed to do with you sitting here in the dark? You look pale. Haven't you managed to sell the government quarter yet?

ANTON: Thekla.

THEKLA: Sorry, it's a secret, I forgot. And apart from that? Spent the day getting mouldy at the office? Or isn't that allowed either?

ANTON: No, the whole time behind my desk.

THEKLA: Overtime?

ANTON: What do you mean?

THEKLA: Sympathy. Because you look green against the window.

ANTON: No, no overtime, I left on time.

MANUELA: Excuse me.

THEKLA: You're still here, excuse me, I was talking to my husband, what was I thinking? Would you like to stay and listen or go home and practise?

MANUELA: I cried all night. I've done everything wrong. Nothing's right anymore, it's not just the piano, suddenly everything's wrong. As if I was stuck in someone else's life. I've lost something and I'm scared I won't get it back.

THEKLA: You lose things as you get older. You must try and cope. I'm getting older myself and putting things behind me – you for example.

MANUELA: I just didn't have anything to compare it with. This is where I belong, here in this room with the tree in the window, I need your heavy perfume and sleepwalker's voice. Christian is ruining me.

THEKLA: Now this creature is crying.

MANUELA: You despise me, I can understand that.

THEKLA: Blow your nose, I'll walk you to the door.

(She takes MANUELA's arm.)

MANUELA: The last couple of days I've been breathing, he says my breathing's wrong and he makes me sing, I'm supposed to open up when I'm playing, I need to connect with my shadow-self and immerse myself before I start playing, but I always fall asleep, he says that's a good sign, but it's just that I can't sleep at night because all that breathing is giving me asthma attacks, and I spend the whole night sitting in an armchair coughing. I'm miserable.

THEKLA: I don't think there's anything left that you can teach me. Drink hot milk with honey and say hello to Christian from me.

(MANUELA has left.)

ANTON: Poor child.

THEKLA: Highly strung.

ANTON: What did the doctor say?

THEKLA: He put cold goo on my belly and I saw her: a little human being in a blizzard-like typhoon.

ANTON: But what did the doctor say?

THEKLA: He asked where you were and why you didn't want to be with me when we look at the child.

ANTON: I'm sorry, I was working.

THEKLA: That's what I told him, but unfortunately it's not true.

ANTON: Why?

THEKLA: I waited so you could come to the doctor's with me, and I sat in the car in front of the main entrance. You said you didn't work late and you left on time.

ANTON: Right.

THEKLA: But I didn't see you. Aschenbrenner limped out the door on time, doubled over, with a yellow face, as if he was having cramps, I got worried and rang the bell and you didn't answer, so I thought conferences and working late and went to the doctor's on my own.

ANTON: I told you not to come to the office anymore.

THEKLA: Because you don't want your colleagues to gawp at our private life, I know, but now I'm wondering if that's the real reason, and what's actually private. You said you had to work. Why did you lie to me? It's embarrassing.

ANTON: It was meant to be a surprise.

THEKLA: That you're lying to me? You left on time but you didn't use the door. Did you fly out the window?

ANTON: I left early and bought you a present. A present. So. So that's it.

THEKLA: A present.

ANTON: Yes. For you. As a surprise.

THEKLA: And where is it?

ANTON: What?

THEKLA: The present. Can I see it?

ANTON: No.

THEKLA: I think I'd like to see it.

ANTON: But you can't.

THEKLA: Why not? Because it's not for me. I'd prefer it if I didn't have to think you're lying.

(ANTON leaves.)

That doesn't mean you have to run away.

(ANTON enters carrying a dug-out birch tree.)

ANTON: Here.

THEKLA: A birch tree.

ANTON: I wanted to put it in the garden to mark the birth. By the pond.

THEKLA: A real birch tree.

ANTON: Yes.

THEKLA: The leaves are trembling.

ANTON: A diaphanous plant, too delicate for the harshness of reality.

THEKLA: Very delicate, those tiny leaves. You must hate me now.

ANTON: I don't hate you.

THEKLA: It was much easier to think you were lying and a stranger to me.

ANTON: Of course, suddenly the curtain is torn open and you see the terrible truth: I've stopped going to work and spend my days in cheap hotels instead, and kill time with magazines, or I sit in car parks and listen to the radio, I eat lunch in motorway service stations and don't drive back to town till the evening so no one sees me, or sometimes I take an exit and stand by a quarry pond or stop by the forest and struggle through the undergrowth, no one even bothers to ask why the sun burns my skin at my desk, apparently no one looks me in the face.

THEKLA: The things you come up with. I'd know.

ANTON: That's good.

THEKLA: I know this dear face, the heaviness in your eyes as if it was all down to you.

ANTON: How's the child?

THEKLA: The child's fine, she's sucking her thumb. That beautiful birch tree. I want it next to our bed tonight and listen to the leaves rustling.

12.

ASCHENBRENNER: The night is relatively calm. In the early hours of the morning there is a detonation, and shortly afterwards the water supply breaks down. While he is inspecting the burst pipes, the chief of command is slain by angry natives and his naked corpse dragged through the streets. The images are blurry, but it's easy to identify the faces, there's dust in their beards and on their skin and they look old. What we don't see is the massacre the soldiers wreak in the crowd before they throw down their weapons and run – there's no ammunition left and the rebels won't fall back despite massive losses, they push on in large numbers into the artillery barrage. At around 6:30 p.m. the western armies pull out of the northern part of the city. For the time being, they say, but the images of soldiers putting up an electric fence in the middle of the street tell me that the northern districts are lost. That means the economic backbone of our corporation is broken. My existence is ruined, I'll end it with the greatest possible decency, there are too many people I don't want to look in the eye after this collapse, myself included. I ask all of us for forgiveness.

13.

(ANTON is sitting on top of the cupboard.)

THEKLA: There he is.

OSKAR: He's in shock.

GRETA: I can see that, but what's he doing on top of the cupboard?

THEKLA: Nothing.

GRETA: Anton?

ANTON: Yes.

GRETA: What are you doing up there?

ANTON: Hello. I'm still a bit weak. The cat next door has caught the fish from our pond again. Now the water's barren.

THEKLA: He's dangling his legs and talking about his carp.

OSKAR: I don't care where he sits. Anton, can you hear me?

ANTON: Loud and clear: you said I don't care where he sits. But since it was a Japanese koi it matters a great deal where he sits, and you should really ask the cat about this.

GRETA: Anton, we need to talk to you.

THEKLA: You'd better come back tomorrow.

OSKAR: There's no time. Anton. It's very simple.

ANTON: It seems terribly complicated to me.

THEKLA: You can't talk to him, he's extremely upset.

ANTON: You can talk but you won't get an answer, fish are dumb. They open and close their jaws and swim back and forth in the water in total silence. You can stroke them, their firm, cold bodies, but do they notice? Hm.

GRETA: What on earth does he want up there?

ANTON: He's looking down at you, he's watching you swim and flap your fins. Here. Something to snap at.

(He sprinkles fish food.)

GRETA: *(To THEKLA.)* Your husband is definitely out of sorts. Oskar, get it over with.

OSKAR: Anton.

ANTON: They're actually terribly stupid, these creatures: when a hand approaches they greedily jump out of the pond, and then they lie on the grass and roll their eyes.

OSKAR: He's not listening. Anton, can you focus your brain for a minute?

THEKLA: Leave him alone, he's ill.

OSKAR: He can't afford to be. Anton.

ANTON: Look at the fat one folding his fins almost like he's trying to be respectable. Here.

(He sprinkles OSKAR with food. GRETA laughs.)

OSKAR: It's brilliant, Anton, all this stuff you're throwing at us.

THEKLA: Anton, what are you doing?

ANTON: *(To THEKLA.)* Nothing. You'd better stay clear of the battlefield.

OSKAR: *(To GRETA.)* Why are you laughing behind my back?

GRETA: The way you're tensed up in front of the cupboard waving your hands. It doesn't suit you: hysteria isn't very flattering.

OSKAR: Nothing I do suits you.

THEKLA: *(To ANTON.)* Please give me the can.

ANTON: No.

GRETA: And get the crumbs out of your hair, it looks ridiculous.

OSKAR: You should be glad there's someone in this room who's more ridiculous than you.

GRETA: *(To THEKLA.)* Now he's baring his heart so we can see it's an old mud hole.

OSKAR: Or does that diminish my appeal as a sex trophy? In that case I'm sorry, because then everyone can see that you're old and shrivelled.

GRETA: You're fast lowering the tone.

OSKAR: You'd better stuff me and hang me on the door so everyone can see you're still capable of attracting young men.

GRETA: You're hardly good for that, you pathetic wreck.

OSKAR: I didn't mean to be crude, it's just that apart from your money there's only thin, stuffy air in my head.

GRETA: That's all right as long as you look beautiful, you silly boy, so be good and get the crumbs from your hair.

OSKAR: You own me skin and bone, if the crumbs bother you, get rid of them yourself, I'll look after your money in the meantime. Anton. Are you listening?

ANTON: Every note. You want to ruin me financially.

OSKAR: Just pull your brain together for a minute, and after that I don't care if you go off with your fish.

ANTON: I never cared about those stupid animals.

OSKAR: It's a delicate matter, but we have to look ahead.

ANTON: When you look back everything seems smaller, have you noticed?

OSKAR: The way things stand now, we no longer have faith in the project.

ANTON: You never did.

GRETA: *(To OSKAR)* Very diplomatic.

(To ANTON.) I just want an expert to have a look at this.

OSKAR: It's too late, I told you that months ago.

GRETA: So now you can gloat, but please do it quietly.

THEKLA: *(To OSKAR)* I can't believe you want to talk about this now.

OSKAR: When else?

THEKLA: He's had a breakdown and needs rest.

OSKAR: Any later and it's too late.

(To ANTON.) There are rumours it was suicide.

ANTON: And I thought the mob killed him. Isn't that what they said on TV?

OSKAR: Aschenbrenner. I'm talking about Aschenbrenner.

ANTON: He's not the type. He's more likely to run amok and take a small town with him.

OSKAR: Apparently he hanged himself in the filing cabinet.

ANTON: I'd know. He doesn't even fit into the filing cabinet, Aschenbrenner deserved a normal heart attack and he got it, read the paper. There's a touching obituary – he earned people's respect and made a difference, and they don't want wreaths, just donations for the heart clinic. So.

OSKAR: Anyway, the situation has changed. The complex is in the middle of the sector and you have to cancel the contract. That's why we need the files you've kept.

GRETA: I didn't say anything about cancelling it, right now we just want the files, then we'll look at the options.

ANTON: I can't cancel it.

OSKAR: Why? That's what it says: in case of natural disasters.

ANTON: The money's gone. Thekla and I are living off it.

OSKAR: Figuratively speaking. But we're serious.

ANTON: How else can you afford a house like this? With a pond and fish in it? Are you still hungry?

(Offers them more fish food.)

No? I'll have a bit more.

(He eats some fish food.)

THEKLA: No, Anton, not that.

GRETA: We're not getting anywhere, the man's got a fever.

ANTON: Right. Had it for months. The man's not well at all. But no one's noticed. And then one day I'm dead and you're still talking at me – you change my underwear every day and buy a wheelchair for my corpse because I can't walk anymore and push me to the table, and you're slightly annoyed that I'm not eating and disappearing a bit more every day. Before I disintegrate completely you might even call the doctor so he can look down my throat and give me an injection, and then he pats me on the back and twists my shoulder in the process and says: you'll be fine, a touch of flu. And you're reassured and put a hot water bottle into bed with my cold corpse and when my head falls off you put it back on and for now you fasten it with two bits of sticky tape, it'll heal.

THEKLA: I told you to leave him alone.

GRETA: I didn't think it was this bad, he was obviously very fond of him.

THEKLA: Like a father.

GRETA: Anton. I don't want to ruin you.

(To THEKLA.) When he can think straight: I need the files on my desk by the end of the week. Then we'll take care of the rest.

ANTON: I'm the rest, and with the rest we'll feed the fish.

GRETA: Right.

(To THEKLA.) Is he going to run the company now?

THEKLA: Probably. Who else is there?

14.

(THEKLA is sitting at the piano playing the same note over and over again.)

ANTON: Thekla?

THEKLA: Yes?

ANTON: I thought you didn't want to go near the piano any more.

THEKLA: That's what I thought, too.

ANTON: I like it when you play.

THEKLA: I don't.

(She keeps repeating the same note.)

ANTON: That note –

THEKLA: I know I'm a disaster. But it's getting better.

ANTON: That's not what I meant. You've been playing nothing but that note for hours.

THEKLA: I want it to grow, to stretch like a muscle. But I lied and it's not getting any better.

ANTON: Maybe it's too difficult to make music with one note.

THEKLA: Why bother dragging myself on stage if I can't get this note right.

ANTON: You don't have to go back on stage anyway, why are you thinking about it again?

(THEKLA stops playing the note.)

THEKLA: I don't know, I'm not supposed to ask any questions, but what's happening down there in that city, at night, when the light is green, I see craters being torn into the ground, and when the sun rises I realise it was a hospital and there's still smoke, why doesn't it stop now it's over, and right in the middle, close to the bus stations, is the complex that's casting a shadow over us, but I'm in a safe place and I'm not supposed to ask what we're doing down there now that I'm having a baby to go with the strawberry fields and the terry-towelling toy and the nursery, why your brain is down there, at dusk people drive through deserted streets in the wrong direction and the chief of command is a pile of bloody flesh, and Aschenbrenner's hanged himself and you're sitting on top of the cupboard, it makes me worry about your future and think about my job, because I might end up having to drag all of us out of this godforsaken hole, and the misery of the community centres is yawning at me.

ANTON: You were shivering as if you were in a cage with beasts of prey, I'm not sending you back there. Soon the families down there will be back in their gardens and they'll be holding drinks in their hands in the mellow evenings and looking at the sky while swarms of mosquitoes whirl over the hedges and swallows shoot through the warm air. Someone's going to rebuild those houses – if your mother won't then someone else will, we don't care where the money comes from.

THEKLA: A couple of days ago I was behind the curtain looking out the window and you were standing in the street behind the car, looking at our house, one hand resting on the roof of the car, eyes empty, as if you were waiting for a voice in your head to say: go in, as if you weren't sure it was your house, as if you were a prisoner of war coming back after fifteen years. I wanted to call out, but suddenly I was afraid that if I startled you and waved it wouldn't be you. For a moment a strange man was standing there.

ANTON: I don't remember.

THEKLA: I'm glad you're not sitting on top of the cupboard any more.

15.

(ASCHENBRENNER is in the cupboard, knocking.)

ANTON: Stop it. I'm deaf.

ASCHENBRENNER: Everyone's gone, you can let me out.

ANTON: I'm not talking to you, you're dead.

ASCHENBRENNER: But you are talking to me. Turn the key.

ANTON: I didn't hang you in the cupboard, you'll have to cope by yourself.

ASCHENBRENNER: The keyhole is big enough, I'll keep an eye on you. I'm offering you a future.

ANTON: Dead people can't talk. You're only in my head.

ASCHENBRENNER: But if you let me I can step out of this cupboard and change your life.

ANTON: You've already changed it, I'm talking to myself, because it's a crisis, what you did to me.

ASCHENBRENNER: Don't be ridiculous. You're wrecking your future.

ANTON: I haven't got a future.

ASCHENBRENNER: I'm your future. Let me out.

(More knocking.)

ANTON: I'm going to go to the door and I'm going to open it, because someone's been knocking at the door for a while now, so now I'm going to open it so the knocking stops, so the knocking in my head stops, I'm now going to open the door where the knocking is coming from.

(He opens the door. MANUELA is standing outside.)

MANUELA: I was just about to leave.

ANTON: If that's what you want.

MANUELA: I thought you were out.

ANTON: Right. Everyone's gone.

MANUELA: But you're in.

ANTON: Our house is empty.

MANUELA: Apart from you.

ANTON: So?

MANUELA: This is when I used to have my lesson.

ANTON: That's in the past.

MANUELA: Can I come in?

(Enters.)

ANTON: The piano stays shut, and so does the cupboard.

MANUELA: It smells nice in here.

ANTON: That's not possible, there's nothing smelly in here. It's the rhododendron.

MANUELA: You've no idea what's stirring inside me.

ANTON: Complete mystery to me.

MANUELA: Paradise lost.

ANTON: Big words.

MANUELA: I thought I had to throw away my crutches and learn how to walk, but then I realised I'd thrown my legs away, and now I'm amputated. I'll wait here for your wife.

ANTON: Bad idea. She doesn't want to see you. Very bad. And I'm not in good shape.

MANUELA: You have to help me.

ANTON: Fortunately, I don't.

MANUELA: I'm a mess.

(She starts to cry. There's a knock.)

ANTON: *(To the cupboard.)* Quiet.

(ANTON fetches two glasses and alcohol. Pours during the following.)

MANUELA: I'm going to throw my life away. I've already thrown it away.

ANTON: You don't know what your life is yet.

MANUELA: If I carry on like this, then I don't want to know.

(A knock.)

ANTON: Stop it.

MANUELA: Help me. I have no future.

ANTON: You haven't even got a past, child. You're obscene.

MANUELA: Talk to your wife.

(There's a knock.)

ANTON: *(Screams.)* Stop it now.

(To MANUELA.) To whom?

MANUELA: So she'll teach me again. You're trembling, you seem very nervous.

ANTON: Piano music gives her a migraine. I don't think she'll risk it for you. Here, have a drink.

MANUELA: You look like a ghost.

ANTON: Exactly, I scare myself when I walk round the corner. Maybe you should buy a window-box or move to the country, put turnips in the ground and build a chicken coop. This city's been on their list for a long time. They'll attack from the west, they always do the train stations first, electricity and gas, once they've wiped out the big factories on the outskirts in advance, they invade the airport, it's their deployment zone, if you stay behind you can watch the grenades tear apart the big avenue downtown and then you can look down into the canals, they blow people out of crowded department stores without prior warning, it's better if you're somewhere else when that happens.

(Screams because there's another knock.) Stop it, this is not the end, there's still some scope, it can get even worse, if you think this is the end you're an optimist.

MANUELA: Are you sure you're all right?

ANTON: No. Unsure.

MANUELA: I'm not thirsty now, I'm leaving, it's getting late outside, my time's almost up anyway.

ANTON: And the darker the night gets the harder they chase you, and in the end there is only flight.

(MANUELA opens the door, THEKLA and OSKAR are standing outside. OSKAR is carrying a bag with live fish.)

THEKLA: What is she doing here?

MANUELA: I'm afraid I had no choice.

THEKLA: Seems like you have no shame.

MANUELA: *(To ANTON.)* And please talk to her.

ANTON: Sometimes you get nervous and you shoot the rocket past the helicopter into space, and then you know that time is against you.

MANUELA: I'm off.

(She leaves.)

THEKLA: What's the girl doing here again?

ANTON: She's showing off with suicide talk. She's silly.

OSKAR: I'll go put the carp in the pond.

(He leaves. There's knocking from the cupboard.)

THEKLA: No sense of distance, that girl. She's like glue, I don't like it.

ANTON: *(Shouting after OSKAR.)* Why don't you go next door and put the fish straight into our neighbours' feeding bowl? Maybe they'll let me drown their cat in our pond in return.

THEKLA: You're so loud.

ANTON: Sorry, there's so much knocking I can't hear a word I'm saying.

(The knocking stops.)

THEKLA: What knocking? I can't hear anything.

ANTON: You can't hear anything?

THEKLA: No. What is it you can hear?

(ANTON listens.)

ANTON: Nothing. Now I can't hear anything either.

THEKLA: Is everything all right?

ANTON: Everything's quiet.

THEKLA: Yes.

ANTON: Quiet. I could stand here and not hear anything for hours – just your face and you in front of the window like this.

THEKLA: I can't do that, I'm already getting tired.

ANTON: It's like when pain stops. I've still got a tingling sensation in my body.

(OSKAR returns.)

OSKAR: The carp are mulling about.

ANTON: Isn't Greta with you? I thought you'd look in the aquarium together and catch the big fish.

OSKAR: Can we have a sensible conversation, is that possible now?

ANTON: I've worn my dressing gown for days and it's wearing me down. And I drink limp tea. Hit me with clear sentences, it'll do me good.

OSKAR: Greta is talking to various lawyers and she's waiting for the files. Until then she won't participate in any fish purchases.

ANTON: That's what you advised her.

OSKAR: She doesn't take my advice.

ANTON: Too modest, I still think it was you.

OSKAR: With those kinds of sums you can't avoid the official route.

ANTON: You're family. Of course I'm very confident and you can do whatever you like, but the fact is that you're bailing out of a project I hand-picked for you after a careful risk-assessment, I didn't make it easy for myself, I can't help it, but I'm hurt by your lack of trust.

ASCHENBRENNER: *(From inside the cupboard.)* Don't tell me you actually believe that rubbish?

ANTON: What?

OSKAR: No one is blaming you for the massacres we read about in the papers every day. We're simply worried about her money.

ANTON: All this excitement is pointless. I've got the money.

ASCHENBRENNER: *(From the cupboard.)* So where is it? Do you mean the wine you've just had or the carpet under your feet or the bed where you lie awake at night?

ANTON: I've got the money and I can pay it back into her account note by note whenever you want –

ASCHENBRENNER: *(From the cupboard.)* Oh really?

OSKAR: If that's true then I don't understand why we still haven't got the files.

ANTON: Only I can't do it that fast. They're complex procedures that take time. You don't have to go waving lawyers at me. We're family.

OSKAR: If everything is in order, then you won't mind a lawyer.

ASCHENBRENNER: *(From inside the cupboard.)* It's just that it's not in order, because chaos has taken root in Anton's world, a black fungus that's dropping spores everywhere, no matter where you look or what you touch, it's contaminated.

ANTON: Shut up.

OSKAR: Me?

ANTON: Don't listen to him.

OSKAR: Who?

THEKLA: What's up with you?

ANTON: This isn't about me, you don't have to torture yourselves because of me. If you haven't got the entrepreneurial instinct – I won't force you.

OSKAR: I know you're very much linked with the project, and I can understand that you're worried about your job. But Aschenbrenner is dead. You'll be running the company soon, you're a free man.

(Laughter from the cupboard.)

ANTON: Like a fish in the air and a bird in the water, exactly. You've worn me out. Tell Greta she'll get the files.

OSKAR: When?

ANTON: Soon.

OSKAR: Why not now?

ANTON: There are some documents in the office I have to get first.

OSKAR: At least give me what you have here.

ANTON: That won't get you anywhere, I'll hand the whole thing over in one go.

OSKAR: Tomorrow.

ANTON: Tomorrow it is. My ears are buzzing.

ASCHENBRENNER: *(From the cupboard.)* I suppose you're hoping you won't survive the night.

ANTON: And the cupboard stays shut.

(He leaves.)

THEKLA: He's still stressed. I'm really worried.

OSKAR: Shall I give you a neck rub?

THEKLA: Excuse me?

OSKAR: I really don't mind.

THEKLA: My neck's not the problem. I wonder why he's so upset.

(OSKAR goes towards the cupboard, intending to open it.)

OSKAR: Who was that girl?

THEKLA: What are you doing?

OSKAR: Nothing, just having a look.

THEKLA: You're not supposed to open the cupboard.

OSKAR: Never mind.

THEKLA: Why are you asking about the girl?

OSKAR: That face. Makes me think silly thoughts.

THEKLA: Silly in what way?

OSKAR: Do you think the files are in there?

THEKLA: No idea. What about the girl?

OSKAR: I just thought – since it was so important.

THEKLA: The girl?

OSKAR: No. That we don't open the cupboard.

THEKLA: I don't know what's in there, I don't care. The girl's my student, if you're interested.

OSKAR: That's all right then.

THEKLA: What's all right then?

OSKAR: I'd just like to have a look in the cupboard.

THEKLA: Why did you ask about my student?

OSKAR: I don't know, I remembered bumping into Anton in town.

THEKLA: When?

OSKAR: Didn't Anton tell you?

THEKLA: What?

OSKAR: I didn't know, I thought you told each other everything.

THEKLA: We do.

OSKAR: That's all right then.

THEKLA: Aha.

OSKAR: Yes.

(Nothing. OSKAR looks at the cupboard.)

THEKLA: You didn't finish.

OSKAR: What?

THEKLA: Apparently you bumped into Anton in town.

OSKAR: Weeks ago, right.

THEKLA: Aha.

OSKAR: That's it, don't look at me like that.

THEKLA: And something troubled you.

OSKAR: Anton is a friend, I don't want to get him into trouble.

THEKLA: What kind of trouble?

OSKAR: That's something between the two of you, I'm keeping out of it.

THEKLA: Out of what?

OSKAR: Your private tension, it's none of my business, I don't like being used.

THEKLA: There is no private tension.

OSKAR: That's all right then.

THEKLA: Aha.

OSKAR: Yes.

(Nothing.)

I don't want to take anything, just have a look inside.

THEKLA: Did he say there was private tension?

OSKAR: He didn't put it like that.

THEKLA: How did he put it?

OSKAR: He was waiting outside a fishmonger's and said he was watching lobsters in order to relax.

THEKLA: I don't know anything about lobsters.

OSKAR: It's not important anyway.

THEKLA: And why did you ask about the girl?

OSKAR: Silly thought, like I said.

THEKLA: I don't see any connection between the girl and the lobsters.

OSKAR: Then everything's great.

THEKLA: Aha.

OSKAR: Yes.

(Nothing. OSKAR looks at the cupboard.)

THEKLA: But you can see a connection.

OSKAR: I don't know, I don't want to say the wrong thing here, so I'd rather not say anything. I wonder if the files are in the cupboard.

THEKLA: In your mind the lobster and girl add up.

OSKAR: You see, that's why I didn't want to say anything, I'm the one who's going to end up looking like an idiot.

THEKLA: You already do.

OSKAR: What?

THEKLA: Look like an idiot. You've already talked too much and said nothing.

OSKAR: I know it's none of my business –

THEKLA: Exactly.

OSKAR: But why does the cupboard have to stay shut?

THEKLA: I want you to tell me, in short sentences, what this is all about, the lobster, the girl, all your silly thoughts.

OSKAR: You're making a big deal out of nothing.

THEKLA: I'll be the judge of that.

OSKAR: It's just that I was wondering – although it's really not important – why Anton's doppelganger needs a room in the hotel by the square.

THEKLA: In the hotel.

OSKAR: I mean, if he's really just interested in the lobster. But you're right, it's none of my business, I just want the files from the cupboard.

THEKLA: A room in the hotel.

OSKAR: By the square, yes.

THEKLA: Aha.

OSKAR: I'm going to open the cupboard.

THEKLA: Do what you want.

(OSKAR opens the cupboard. It's empty.)

OSKAR: Strange.

THEKLA: Anton doesn't have a doppelganger.

16.

ANTON: What are you doing in my forest?

ASCHENBRENNER: It was only a matter of time until you showed up here.

ANTON: I chose this place because there are no people, just a hawk circling now and then.

ASCHENBRENNER: You can't claim a whole forest to yourself. I've been hanging out here longer than you.

ANTON: I've been on the battlefield for weeks and never saw you.

ASCHENBRENNER: I ordered this field, put down the foundations, everything's ready for our big project.

ANTON: You're fast. I thought you'd still be in the cupboard.

ASCHENBRENNER: Do you think someone of my stature ever rests? We'll realise our vision in this place.

ANTON: You're forgetting that you threw me out the window and into the kitchen waste.

ASCHENBRENNER: You're tailor-made for this challenge. This place is going to be an open-air museum of mankind. In the old days they didn't find the men who had hanged themselves in the forest until the autumn, when the leaves had dropped and cleared the view of the branches, or one of them had a crutch and put it against the trunk, and the wanderer knew: there's someone with a crooked leg hanging up there. From now on, when you take the exit to the forest, there'll be a passport nailed to each trunk so you know who's up there, and if that's not enough we can put up their tax returns as well. Then the visitor can walk from tree to tree in our museum of mankind, arms behind his back, and there'll be feet floating around his head and gently stirring in the wind. Everything's ready. Now hand me your passport.

ANTON: I have a wife, we're having a baby.

ASCHENBRENNER: You're whining again. Here.

(He gives him a clothesline.)

ANTON: It's a clothesline.

ASCHENBRENNER: It was the only thing I could find at your place. Hang yourself out to dry. For short distances you can also use your tie, in case you want to copy me again.

ANTON: I'm not ready, I want to see my child first.

ASCHENBRENNER: Your wife, your child – it's only got a fake future, you're aware of that, aren't you? What's going to happen when everything collapses?

ANTON: I don't know.

ASCHENBRENNER: You need to be professional about this. Your passport, please.

17.

(THEKLA, ANTON and ASCHENBRENNER are sitting at the table, there's lobster for dinner.)

THEKLA: You've set an extra plate. Are you expecting someone?

ANTON: Extra?

THEKLA: Is Manuela coming round?

ANTON: Manuela?

THEKLA: I'm taking the plate away now.

(She takes ASCHENBRENNER's plate.)

ASCHENBRENNER: I wasn't really hungry anyway.

ANTON: I guess I was thinking about the child.

ASCHENBRENNER: Clever.

THEKLA: Sure. And? Do you like the lobster meat?

ANTON: I haven't tried it yet.

THEKLA: The lobster's from the square.

ANTON: Aha.

THEKLA: The shop where they pull them out of the water while they're still alive.

ANTON: So that they're fresh.

THEKLA: I stood by the window for a while and wondered which one would have to die.

ANTON: Yes. Lobsters make you philosophical.

THEKLA: You've noticed, have you?

ANTON: I would imagine. In the face of death.

THEKLA: How calmly they float on death row.

ANTON: They don't know where they are. They're happy.

THEKLA: Stupid animals.

ANTON: Let's eat them.

THEKLA: A shop on the square, you've probably been there.

ANTON: I don't go to the square very often.

THEKLA: Aha.

(THEKLA gets up.)

ANTON: Where are you going?

(THEKLA leaves.)

ASCHENBRENNER: It's going to get unsavoury now because you don't know when it's enough and instead you stare at your wife, who has no future. You could have been floating among the trees by now, with a fresh breeze around your legs, but you're a sentimental wimp.

ANTON: I can't hear what you're saying, you're just in my head, and you haven't even got a plate.

(THEKLA returns with the birch tree, which she's cut down.)

THEKLA: There.

ANTON: What's this?

THEKLA: Cut down.

ANTON: Who did that?

THEKLA: Me. I cut down the birch tree.

ANTON: No.

THEKLA: Yes. This afternoon.

ANTON: You wouldn't do that.

THEKLA: No, I wouldn't, but I did. You'd never lie or cheat on me either.

ANTON: No.

THEKLA: But you did. Anything's possible, like on the first day, and everything's assailing me and there's no shelter. It's possible for a birch tree to stand outside the window like an insult and I fetch the saw from the shed and cut it down so it's over. It rustled when it sank into the grass. Wasn't very loud.

ANTON: That's the birch tree for our child.

THEKLA: I know your ways now, the phone where I call you at the office every lunchtime and send you kisses, it's not in your office but in a hotel room on the square, I saw you disappear into it today.

ANTON: What, how do you know –?

THEKLA: How am I supposed to answer that when I don't even know who I'm talking to, I look at you and I don't see anything, you haven't got a face anymore, everything's gone, it's like you shaved the face from your head this morning. Then at lunchtime you disappeared into the hotel, I want you to explain that to me.

ASCHENBRENNER: You can't explain anything, I've reserved the oak tree for you, no one's going to understand, you're mine.

ANTON: I can't explain it.

THEKLA: Because you're seeing a woman.

ANTON: No.

THEKLA: A student of mine.

ANTON: No.

THEKLA: Then tell me what you get up to in there.

ANTON: I can't.

THEKLA: Because there's a woman.

ASCHENBRENNER: Just admit it, doesn't matter if it's not true.

ANTON: No.

THEKLA: Of course it's a woman, what else would it be?

ANTON: Nothing.

THEKLA: You rent a hotel room for nothing.

ANTON: Yes.

THEKLA: And you think I'm going to believe that?

ANTON: No.

THEKLA: Then tell me why you need the hotel room.

ANTON: To hang out.

THEKLA: With a woman.

ANTON: No.

THEKLA: Yes. With a woman. It's terrible: it all adds up, the last couple of months, you acting erratic, that you don't speak for days on end, it all makes sense now.

ANTON: It makes sense, but it's nonsense.

THEKLA: And the way my student has changed. I'm almost relieved now that I know.

ANTON: You don't know anything, everything you're thinking is wrong.

THEKLA: Then tell me what's right.

ANTON: I can't.

THEKLA: Because I'm right.

ANTON: No.

THEKLA: So it is my student?

ASCHENBRENNER: Admit it and that's it.

ANTON: No.

THEKLA: Why did you meet here when you've got the hotel room? Wasn't once a day enough?

ANTON: I'm always alone in that room.

THEKLA: Why?

ANTON: I can't tell you that.

THEKLA: Because you're with a woman.

ASCHENBRENNER: Admit it, or do you want to slam the fork into your throat while she's watching?

ANTON: No.

THEKLA: Yes. Why do you need a hotel room in bright daylight?

ANTON: I can't tell you.

THEKLA: Because I'm right.

ANTON: Please, don't ask me to explain.

THEKLA: You can stop trying to explain, it's clear as daylight.

ANTON: I've got the room against the rain. When I've been outside and walking for hours I get tired, once I stopped in the car park in the industrial estate and fell into a deep sleep behind the wheel, and when I woke up there was a beaten-up face with a pasty forehead pressed against the window, and it was staring in at me with inflamed eyes, so I went to the hotel.

THEKLA: A pasty face. Aha.

(There's a knock.)

ANTON: Exactly, I lost my job on the twentieth of March, and I have to go somewhere, I like spending time in the forest when the sun shines through the leaves, sometimes I'm there for hours watching hawks, but I'm a human being and I need a room when it rains, the noise when the key turns in the lock, the locked door. That's why I need a hotel.

THEKLA: That's the most ridiculous thing I've ever heard.

ANTON: It really is ridiculous, that's why I never told you, but now you know. No woman, there's only you.

THEKLA: We could have talked about everything, I'm fond of you and I'm having your baby. But you keep on lying, as if things weren't bad enough, it's obvious that you're cheating on me,

(She starts to cry.)

that you're telling me all this nonsense hoping I'll be stupid enough to believe you – you have to understand that I can't live like this.

(It's still knocking, so she goes to the door.)

ANTON: Don't open it.

THEKLA: Why not?

ANTON: Please. I need more time.

THEKLA: What for? You're lying to me and I've nothing more to say.

(She opens the door. GRETA and OSKAR.)

OSKAR: We've come to get the files.

ANTON: It's not a good time.

OSKAR: It never is.

GRETA: I can't wait any longer.

ANTON: I'm indisposed right now.

OSKAR: Give us the files and we'll go.

GRETA: I'm not interested in your private situation, today I'm here on business.

OSKAR: What's the birch tree doing on the floor?

ANTON: That's difficult to explain. I'd like you to leave.

THEKLA: I cut it down, we don't need the tree any more.

GRETA: Your relationship has definitely reached a critical point if you've started dragging the garden into your house. I don't want to know any of this, Anton, I must ask you to give me the files, I'm afraid I have no choice.

ANTON: Can't you come back later? Can't you see that–

THEKLA: I won't be here later.

GRETA: There's no time for discussions right now, my lawyer is waiting.

ANTON: Just give me half an hour.

GRETA: I'm afraid we don't have that long.

ANTON: Then I have no choice.

GRETA: No.

OSKAR: The files, or we'll see each other in court.

ANTON: We won't see each other ever again. I'll bring this matter to a decent end. I'll go and get the files.

OSKAR: You'd better.

ANTON: Wait here. I'll be right back.

(He kisses THEKLA's forehead.)

THEKLA: Don't touch me.

ANTON: I'm sorry.

(He exits.)

OSKAR: Well then.

GRETA: Get rid of the tree, it's not civilised.

OSKAR: This whole thing is embarrassing.

THEKLA: Shut up.

OSKAR: I'm just saying I'm not pleased with the way things have turned out.

THEKLA: I said I don't want to hear anything.

GRETA: Be quiet and get the plant out of here.

OSKAR: Right.

(OSKAR drags the tree outside.)

GRETA: Here, blow your nose.

(Gives THEKLA a handkerchief.)

You look terrible.

THEKLA: Look the other way if it bothers you.

GRETA: Letting yourself go like this.

THEKLA: If I'd let myself go the crockery would be on the floor by now.

GRETA: You don't have to exaggerate. Aren't you going to eat the lobster?

THEKLA: Help yourself if you're hungry.

GRETA: It's a precious animal, you shouldn't let it go to waste.

(GRETA eats. Nothing for a while. OSKAR returns.)

OSKAR: Has he brought the files yet?

GRETA: He's still upstairs.

OSKAR: I'm glad this thing is over, it was too risky from the start.

GRETA: I know, we've been through all this, 'you should have listened to me, I told you', I've had enough.

OSKAR: It's about respect, that's all.

GRETA: Shut up. I wonder what he's doing.

OSKAR: *(To THEKLA.)* Shall I give you a neck rub while we're waiting?

(THEKLA stares at him.)

GRETA: You'd better check what Anton is up to and give him a hand.

OSKAR: With pleasure.

(He exits. GRETA eats.)

GRETA: Is there any wine left?

THEKLA: Of course.

(She pours a glass for her. GRETA drinks and continues to eat. Nothing for a while. OSKAR returns, points with his finger.)

OSKAR: Anton.

THEKLA: What?

OSKAR: He's hung himself upstairs. He's hanging from the ceiling with a clothesline.

THEKLA: Anton.

18.

(MANUELA is playing the piano. THEKLA is sitting behind her. Only music for a while, then a mistake.)

THEKLA: Start again from there.

MANUELA: Yes.

THEKLA: And calm down, your fingers are still too feverish.

MANUELA: I'm sorry, I'm nervous.

THEKLA: It'll pass.

MANUELA: Yes.

(She continues to play. GRETA and OSKAR come out of ANTON's room, OSKAR is carrying two bags.)

OSKAR: We're all set.

(MANUELA stops playing.)

THEKLA: Don't let them bother you.

(MANUELA resumes playing.)

GRETA: Your things are already in the car.

THEKLA: The piano as well?

OSKAR: We'll get the furniture later.

THEKLA: It's an instrument, not a piece of furniture.

GRETA: In any case, you have to get up now and put your coat on.

THEKLA: I have to?

GRETA: *(To OSKAR.)* Go and put that in the boot, we'll be right there.

OSKAR: Yes.

(He exits.)

GRETA: *(To MANUELA.)* You can stop, the piano lesson's over.

(MANUELA stops.)

THEKLA: Keep playing.

GRETA: *(To THEKLA.)* We talked everything through.

(MANUELA starts playing.)

THEKLA: Right, I'll come to your place and have a foam bath to combat exertion.

GRETA: For example.

THEKLA: And I'll have breakfast at lunchtime and wear a pastel-coloured dressing gown and hold a small dog on my lap.

GRETA: Whatever you want.

THEKLA: No. Whatever you want. You own this house. The garden, the pond, the piano, what I'm wearing, the protein in my body, the fat, the chalk in my bones: it's all paid for with your money.

GRETA: If it's an investment that helps save you now that's fine with me.

THEKLA: You bought our life. I'd like mine back.

GRETA: You can't afford it.

(MANUELA stops playing.)

MANUELA: I'm sorry.

THEKLA: What?

MANUELA: It's impossible to concentrate. If I have to try not to hear your voices the whole time, I end up not hearing anything and playing like a machine. I'm sorry.

THEKLA: *(To GRETA.)* I have to ask you to leave. You're bothering my student.

GRETA: Think about it. You have no future here. The place is contaminated with memories. It won't be long before the poisoned air starts to suffocate you. My house has warm walls and sunlight on the parquet. Don't be proud. My door is open.

THEKLA: Thanks.

(GRETA leaves.)

THEKLA: *(To MANUELA.)* I'm sorry. Start again.

(MANUELA plays. Music for a while.)

ANTON: Thekla.

THEKLA: *(To MANUELA.)* Keep playing.

ANTON: Thekla.

(THEKLA goes over to ANTON.)

THEKLA: I can hear you, Anton.

ANTON: Thekla, it's stopped.

THEKLA: Be quiet, Anton, everything's all right, you shouldn't talk with that throat.

ANTON: It's stopped.

THEKLA: You need to get some more sleep.

ANTON: But –

THEKLA: Keep quiet, you don't have to worry anymore. They just came by to get the papers.

ANTON: It's over.

THEKLA: We'll lose the house and everything, but you won't lose me. I'm not sure yet how it's going to work, but it will, I'm sure of that.

ANTON: It's stopped. He's gone now.

THEKLA: You don't have to think that anymore. We'll watch our daughter grow, and the bigger she gets the smaller we'll get, till one day we disappear and everything belongs to her. That's what it's all about, that's the whole purpose, and soon we'll be a part of all that.

ANTON: Aschenbrenner is gone at last. I don't hear him any more. Not a sound. Everything's quiet.

THEKLA: Yes. Quiet.

ANTON: Quiet at last.

THEKLA: You have to sleep now, we'll talk about everything else later.

ASCHENBRENNER: At midnight local time, the western armies abandon the city. A temporary measure they claim, a strategic withdrawal, but the images of soldiers pushing helicopters from aircraft carriers – in order to make room for fleeing comrades – leave no doubt that the area is lost forever. Today we're faced with a historic challenge: the development of several thousand square kilometres of real estate in hitherto uninhabited territory. The scientists will supply water, everything else – atmosphere, seas, lakes, rivers – will come: life has started from water once before. Because of the change in radiation, people will grow a skin of gold, and shimmering figures will move through cities of red stone, everything's red there, the whole planet, and there's not just one sun in the yellow sky, but other stars as well, they're moving in a vast, formidable system, and this old earth looks radiant in the distance, it's so beautiful and so far away. Here, history has entrusted the investor with a piece of the world that looks virginal in the glow of the morning stars.

The End.

PERPLEX

Perplex was first performed at the Schaubühne am Lehniner Platz on 20 November 2010, directed by Marius von Mayenburg.

The first English-language production was at Sydney Theatre Company's Wharf 1 Theatre on 31 March 2014, directed by Sarah Giles.

Characters

EVA

JUDITH

ROBERT

SEBASTIAN

The names of the actors in the original production were: Eva Meckbach, Judith Engel, Robert Beyer and Sebastian Schwarz. They were kind enough to let me use their first names for this play. It's up to each new production to decide whether they want to use these names as well or to substitute them with the names of their actors. The surname Eckels should be kept.

Location:
A living room in a single-family house. A kitchen door on the left, a door to the hallway on the right.

(ROBERT enters from the hallway, he's carrying two suitcases. Puts them down.)

ROBERT: Right.

(He stands between the suitcases, looks around.)

Any mail?

(Nothing. He repeats, without raising his voice.)

Any mail?

(Nothing. He takes off his jacket, sits on the sofa. Looks around. Shouts angrily.)

I asked you a question, Eva.

(Nothing. He gets up and opens a window. Calm again.)

This place needs some fresh air.

(EVA enters from the hallway, a parcel under her arm, a pile of letters and postcards in her hand. She's staring at an opened letter on top of the pile.)

EVA: Listen, Robert –

(She stops, stares at the letter. Puts the parcel on the coffee table.)

ROBERT: No one opened a window the whole time we were gone.

EVA: Robert, listen, I'm just wondering –

(ROBERT returns from the window and bumps into the coffee table.)

ROBERT: *(Surprised.)* Ouch.

EVA: Did you send the money for the electricity?

ROBERT: *(Rubs his shin.)* What electricity?

EVA: The electric company. Did you pay the bill.

ROBERT: What do you mean the electric company? I just banged my leg on this thing.

EVA: Because apparently they've cut it off.

ROBERT: *(Examines his shin.)* I always get a bruise.

(EVA goes to the light switch, flicks it on and off, nothing happens.)

EVA: You see?

ROBERT: Yes. No light. But you don't pay the electric company for your electricity.

EVA: Well – you certainly didn't.

ROBERT: They can't just turn off our electricity.

EVA: No?

(She angrily flicks the switch.)

ROBERT: Why me, anyway?

EVA: There are two reminders.

ROBERT: Why do *I* have to pay the electricity bill?

EVA: Because you said you'd take care of it.

ROBERT: You're making that up.

EVA: Robert. We no longer have any electricity. We're sitting in the dark.

ROBERT: It's light.

EVA: Because the sun is shining. When it goes down it'll be dark.

ROBERT: That's because the earth turns, what do you want me to do about it?

EVA: Pay your fucking bills.

ROBERT: Aha. My bills.

EVA: If you say you're going to do it, do it. Otherwise

I'd rather do it myself in the first place.

ROBERT: How am I supposed to do it when I'm on holiday? And anyway, why didn't Sebastian and Judith tell us that we got these reminders.

EVA: Because they don't read our letters.

ROBERT: They're here every day watering your stupid flowers, they could be a bit more vigilant, no?

EVA: And tear open our letters?

ROBERT: From the electric company, if that's what it says in big letters, electricity, what's private about that, you tear it open, you have a look, you think, it's the least you can do before the electricity gets turned off.

EVA: Calm down.

ROBERT: What?

EVA: Calm down.

ROBERT: I don't need to calm down, you're the one who should calm down: flick, flick, we're in the dark.

EVA: My flowers aren't stupid.

ROBERT: This isn't about your flowers.

EVA: They're your flowers too.

ROBERT: No.

(Nothing.)

Did they at least water them?

(EVA goes to the kitchen to check.)

I wouldn't be surprised. Sebastian always says sure, I'll take care of it, no problem, but then he's so busy thinking he's adorable that he forgets everything else. He lives in a bubble.

(Nothing.)

Eva?

(Nothing.)

Eva?

(ROBERT is getting louder.)

I said he lives in a bubble.

(Nothing. He shouts.) In a bubble, get it?

(Nothing. He starts towards the kitchen. EVA returns. She's carrying a large potted plant.)

EVA: What did you say?

ROBERT: I said he lives in a bubble.

EVA: Who?

ROBERT: I don't know. Sebastian.

EVA: What makes you say that?

ROBERT: No idea.

(About the plant.) What's that? It's still alive.

EVA: Yes. Did you put it there?

ROBERT: Me? Where?

EVA: I don't know this plant.

ROBERT: Me neither. I don't know any plants. You're the botanical one.

EVA: I've never seen it before. This plant is completely unfamiliar to me. I had no idea a plant like this even existed. I just went into the kitchen and there it was, alive.

ROBERT: You probably planted some kind of pip and while we were on holiday it put down roots and grew into this plant.

EVA: No.

(Nothing.)

ROBERT: What's in the parcel?

EVA: How would I know, I haven't opened it.

ROBERT: Who's it from?

EVA: Robert, you have a look. Open it, if you want, and look inside.

(Nothing.)

ROBERT: I think I'll go and unpack my suitcase.

(Starts to leave.)

EVA: While it's still light.

ROBERT: What?

EVA: Because when it starts to get dark you won't be able to see.

(ROBERT crashes into the coffee table.)

ROBERT: *(Surprised.)* Ouch.

EVA: You see.

ROBERT: What?

EVA: You can't see anything.

ROBERT: I can see everything. Why is this stupid table always in the way?

EVA: So now the table is stupid.

ROBERT: I asked you a question.

EVA: Just because you didn't pay the bill.

ROBERT: What bill?

EVA: The electricity bill. Because you didn't pay it you can't switch on the light and crash into the furniture in the dark, and then you call it stupid. You're the one who's stupid.

(ROBERT stares at her, suddenly starts to laugh.)

What's with the laughter?

(ROBERT laughs.)

Why the stupid laughter?

ROBERT: It's just the way you're standing there, with your stupid pot, in the middle of the room.

(EVA looks down at herself.)

EVA: Do I look stupid?

(ROBERT nods, he's laughing so hard he can't speak. EVA starts to laugh as well.)

Stupid, right?

(ROBERT nods, sheds tears of laughter.)

ROBERT: Stupid.

(EVA laughs. ROBERT laughs. SEBASTIAN and JUDITH are standing in the room.)

JUDITH: Looks like you're having fun.

(EVA and ROBERT stop laughing.)

(To SEBASTIAN.) Look, they're laughing.

SEBASTIAN: *(Grins.)* No they're not.

EVA: *(Euphoric greeting.)* Sebastian. Judith.

(She puts the potted plant on the coffee table and hugs them.)

ROBERT: Of course. You have a key.

EVA: We were just talking about you.

SEBASTIAN: Only good things, I hope.

ROBERT: Exactly, that's what you always say when people tell you they've been talking about you.

EVA: *(To SEBASTIAN.)* Only good things, exactly.

ROBERT: Hello Sebastian, do you always say what people always say?

JUDITH: Why, what did you say?

SEBASTIAN: *(Sits down.)* So, how was your holiday?

(The others gradually sit down as well.)

ROBERT: And another one.

EVA: What?

ROBERT: He just said another one of those things you always say when someone comes back from a holiday: how was your holiday?

EVA: Lovely. It was lovely.

ROBERT: Now you're starting as well. Lovely. That's what people always say. How was your holiday? It was lovely.

EVA: *(To ROBERT.)* Cut it out, will you?

JUDITH: So it wasn't lovely?

ROBERT: Yes, hello Judith, do you really want to know? Shall we get the projector and show you two thousand slides?

SEBASTIAN: Did you bring a projector?

EVA: What do you mean – bring?

ROBERT: Disregarding for a moment that we can't show you any slides because the electricity has been turned off.

JUDITH: I was wondering about that. Why are you sitting in the dark?

SEBASTIAN: Exactly, put the light on.

ROBERT: *(To SEBASTIAN.)* Put the light on, put the light on. Go ahead, you put the light on.

EVA: Robert didn't pay the bill.

ROBERT: Robert didn't pay the bill, Robert didn't pay the bill.

EVA: *Did* you pay the bill? I'd offer you a coffee, but the coffee machine has no power.

ROBERT: Because Robert didn't pay the bill. And no one told him about the reminders.

SEBASTIAN: I'm sure it's not that bad.

(He gets up and switches on the light.)

EVA: Oh, how did you – ?

SEBASTIAN: Like this.

(Demonstrates, flicks the light switch.)

This is a switch, and when you press it like this –

ROBERT: *(A moronic lisp.)* Is that right? A switch? Flick, flick. Incredible.

JUDITH: Why was Robert meant to pay the bill?

ROBERT: Yeah, exactly, why?

SEBASTIAN: What I was wondering: are there really that many snails under water?

ROBERT: *(Sober.)* Snails.

EVA: Mainly black ones.

SEBASTIAN: And the natives throw them on the barbecue?

EVA: They go up and down the beach and sell them from their baskets.

JUDITH: Would you like a coffee?

EVA: I'm sorry.

ROBERT: Yes, now that the current is flowing and everything.

EVA: I'll go and make one.

JUDITH: You don't have to do that, I'll go. Sebastian, darling?

SEBASTIAN: With milk.

JUDITH: Of course.

SEBASTIAN and JUDITH: *(Together.)* And two lumps of sugar.

(They laugh.)

SEBASTIAN: And one of those biscuits on the side.

ROBERT: No sugar for me, thanks.

EVA: Don't you want to give Judith a hand?

ROBERT: Don't *you* want to give Judith a hand?

SEBASTIAN: I definitely don't want to give Judith a hand.

(He laughs.)

In case anyone's interested.

EVA: Under the Southern sun Robert has regressed to the level of a toddler, these are the terrible twos.

ROBERT: Delightful, isn't he? Our little Robert.

(He sucks his thumb. JUDITH looks at him.)

JUDITH: So no sugar for you. Eva?

EVA: It doesn't matter.

JUDITH: It doesn't matter doesn't exist.

EVA: The way you're having it.

JUDITH: I'm not having anything.

EVA: In that case sit down and I'll go.

(She starts to get up.)

JUDITH: *(Without any sense of humour.)* Stop it. As long as your feet are under my table I'm in charge of the coffee.

(EVA laughs.)

EVA: That's funny.

(JUDITH looks at her, laughs as well and goes into the kitchen.)

SEBASTIAN: Back to the underwater world.

EVA: Take your thumb out of your mouth, Robert.

ROBERT: The most beautiful thing was a diving bird that had air bubbles coming out of its plumage. It was a precise, choreographed movement of inimitable elegance.

SEBASTIAN: You go snorkeling in a coral reef and the most beautiful thing you see is a duck?

(In the kitchen several cups go crashing onto the tiles.)

EVA: And now she's smashing our china.

SEBASTIAN: Are you all right, darling?

JUDITH: *(From the kitchen.)* Everything's fine. They were hideous anyway.

EVA: Oh really?

SEBASTIAN: She's never liked the china. She throws one piece after the other onto the tiles so she can get a new set. Who put that plant there?

EVA: Yes, that. What kind of plant is it?

SEBASTIAN: It belongs in the kitchen.

(JUDITH enters from the kitchen carrying a dustpan with broken china.)

JUDITH: We really need to have a word with the cleaning lady.

SEBASTIAN: What is it this time?

JUDITH: I can't find the rubbish bin. Unbelievable, isn't it?

EVA: Under the sink, the lid goes up when you open the door.

JUDITH: You'd think so, wouldn't you? But the cleaning lady has thrown the rubbish bin away. She throws all the rubbish bins away. She thinks they're rubbish. Excuse me.

(With panache, she throws the pieces of china under the sofa.)

EVA: Judith? What are you doing?

ROBERT: She's throwing pieces of china under the sofa.

EVA: I can see that.

ROBERT: Then why did you ask?

EVA: It was a rhetorical question, Robert, because I'm stunned.

(She reaches under the sofa and pulls out a heap of rubbish, some of it in plastic bags.)

JUDITH: What choice do I have?

EVA: You're just throwing all your rubbish under the sofa?

ROBERT: Eva, as you can see: she's throwing all her rubbish under the sofa. Why do keep asking such daft questions?

EVA: Robert, shut up. I don't know about you, but I'm going to clear this away.

(She starts to clear away the rubbish.)

JUDITH: Don't. You don't have to clear away our rubbish.

EVA: I agree, but obviously –

SEBASTIAN: It's just that the cleaning lady keeps throwing the rubbish bins away.

JUDITH: *(To Sebastian.)* Did you put that plant there?

SEBASTIAN: Wasn't me, I'm puzzled by it as well.

JUDITH: It belongs in the kitchen.

EVA: Actually, it doesn't.

JUDITH: No?

EVA: Actually it doesn't even belong in the flat.

JUDITH: You think.

ROBERT: I've got it.

EVA: What? What have you got?

ROBERT: The rubbish.

EVA: What about it?

ROBERT: That's why it smells stuffy.

JUDITH: Oh really.

SEBASTIAN: You're under the impression that it smells stuffy.

ROBERT: Yes. From the moment I walked in. Isn't that what I said, Eva?

EVA: What did you say, Robert? You're getting on my nerves.

ROBERT: I walked through the door and I said, Jesus, Christ Almighty, it stinks, it reeks of –

EVA: Of what? Robert, you're talking rubbish.

ROBERT: Exactly, rubbish, that's what I said.

JUDITH: You're of the opinion that the flat stinks.

ROBERT: Yes, have a sniff.

SEBASTIAN: Is that why you put the plant here?

ROBERT: I don't do plants, that's Eva.

SEBASTIAN: So it can spread a more pleasant smell or what?

JUDITH: Robert, the plant is not in bloom. It doesn't smell of anything.

SEBASTIAN: No smell.

ROBERT: Forget the plant for a minute: obviously what's causing the stench is the rubbish you're throwing under your sofa.

EVA: Robert, it's not their sofa, it's our sofa.

ROBERT: Listen, Eva –

EVA: Yes, Robert?

ROBERT: Eva, what really interests me is: don't you think it's time you said thank you?

EVA: To you? What for?

ROBERT: Don't you want to thank Judith and Sebastian for watering your plants?

(JUDITH and SEBASTIAN think this is funny. They laugh.)

EVA: Is this meant to be a joke?

ROBERT: No.

EVA: They smash our china, read our letters, throw their rubbish under our sofa and replace our plants. What am I supposed to thank them for?

ROBERT: They didn't read the letters, did they. Did you read our letters?

EVA: Where, for example, is my basil?

SEBASTIAN: I'm tired, darling, I think I'm going to have a nap.

EVA: Did you let my basil die?

JUDITH: Don't take this the wrong way, but it's been a long day, we haven't had a holiday like you. Maybe you could come back another time.

SEBASTIAN: With a projector, snails and all the details. But today –

JUDITH: Today it's really getting a bit late.

SEBASTIAN: No offence. Do you want me to call you a taxi?

EVA: A taxi?

JUDITH: Yes, darling, go on.

EVA: We don't want a taxi.

SEBASTIAN: In that case –

EVA: Why would we –

(SEBASTIAN kisses EVA's cheeks, pats ROBERT's back.)

SEBASTIAN: *(To JUDITH.)* I'm going to have a shower.

(He leaves.)

JUDITH: I'll just clear up the pigsty in the kitchen, and then I'll come to bed as well, darling.

(To EVA and ROBERT.) You know your way out, don't you.

(Kisses their cheeks. JUDITH exits to the kitchen with the dustpan. Nothing.)

ROBERT: Right. Let's go.

EVA: Where did he go?

ROBERT: To the bathroom. To bed. Who cares.

EVA: But –

ROBERT: Hmm?

EVA: Isn't it our bed?

(ROBERT doesn't know, he shrugs.)

Shouldn't we be sleeping in it?

ROBERT: Apparently not.

EVA: Yes, but I wonder –

ROBERT: I know exactly what you mean. But apparently –

(He looks around, goes to the light switch, flicks the light off and on a couple of times.)

EVA: I don't know this plant.

ROBERT: What I don't understand is –

(He looks at the coffee table.)

EVA: And we used to have a cat.

ROBERT: Didn't this have a glass top?

EVA: Where did he go? Moritz. Striped. With a bowl in the kitchen.

ROBERT: This table. I used to look at my feet when we had guests and I was eating peanuts. Through the top. No?

EVA: Or did he get run over by a car?

(The doorbell rings. They don't know what to do. There's another ring. SEBASTIAN enters, naked, dries his hair, looks out the window.)

SEBASTIAN: Your taxi.

JUDITH: *(Calls out as she enters.)* Get the door, darling?

(Sees EVA and ROBERT, gets a fright.)

JUDITH: Jesus, Christ Almighty, you gave me a start.

ROBERT: Sorry.

JUDITH: What are you still doing here?

EVA: We've already left.

SEBASTIAN: They've pretty much already left.

ROBERT: Already left. Look, I'm just picking up our suitcases.

(He picks up their suitcases. There's another ring.)

EVA: And we've already left.

JUDITH: Such a start.

ROBERT: Left.

EVA: Left.

(They leave. JUDITH needs to sit down. ROBERT returns with his suitcases.)

JUDITH: Sebastian?

ROBERT: *(Almost at the same time as JUDITH.)* Sebastian?

SEBASTIAN: Yes, darling?

ROBERT: Sebastian, what I meant to say: you're not wearing anything.

SEBASTIAN: That's more convenient when you have a shower.

ROBERT: I see.

(He starts to leave. Returns.)

ROBERT: Did you just call me darling?

SEBASTIAN: No, Robert.

ROBERT: Okay.

(He leaves.)

JUDITH: Has he left?

SEBASTIAN: You know what I've just realised?

JUDITH: I got such a start. I came out of the kitchen and the two of them were standing right in the living room. Like two hangmen. I like them, but when they show up without telling us first, it makes me want to eliminate them.

SEBASTIAN: That's understandable, but you know what I've just realised?

JUDITH: You've realised something.

SEBASTIAN: Yes.

JUDITH: Don't you want to put something on first?

SEBASTIAN: No, I've just discovered the secret of how the species developed. In the shower.

JUDITH: Do tell, that sounds so exciting, but please put something on.

SEBASTIAN: It's possible that animals and human beings as we know them weren't created by God.

JUDITH: No?

SEBASTIAN: No, they developed over millions of years through genetic malformations.

JUDITH: Malformations?

SEBASTIAN: Just imagine, at first human beings only had one eye, that was enough, they could see everything. But then, suddenly, a freak is born and it has two eyes. Everyone thinks: gross. But the freak can see more and he sees the sabre-toothed tiger first, and the freak runs away and the normal ones with one eye get eaten.

JUDITH: By the sabre-toothed tiger.

SEBASTIAN: The sabre-toothed tiger is an example. The freak mates with another two-eyed freak –

JUDITH: Which has also survived the sabre-toothed tiger –

SEBASTIAN: Exactly, because all the one-eyed ones have been eaten, and that's why we all have four eyes.

JUDITH: Four eyes?

SEBASTIAN: Exactly, two plus two –

(JUDITH looks at him. SEBASTIAN corrects himself.)

Two eyes, that's why we have two eyes, all of us.

JUDITH: You mean we're actually freaks?

SEBASTIAN: Yes, isn't it terrific? There was this big casting. With death and sex. Death chooses who gets kicked out and sex who makes it to the next round. We are what we are because of death and sex.

JUDITH: Aha?

SEBASTIAN: Death and sex. What do you think of my theory?

JUDITH: But Sebastian –

SEBASTIAN: I know, it's difficult to accept that you weren't created by God in the Garden of Eden and that your grandfather was a monkey –

JUDITH: Sebastian, this theory already exists.

SEBASTIAN: No.

JUDITH: It's Darwin.

SEBASTIAN: Who?

JUDITH: Natural selection. That's what the big casting is called.

SEBASTIAN: Nono, I've just come up with it. In the shower. Those who escape death have sex –

JUDITH: I get the idea. It's Darwin. Not you.

SEBASTIAN: Why do you keep saying Darwin, it's genetic, death and sex, it's a global genetic optimisation programme, and the crazy thing is, we're all participating in it when we – *(Hip movement.)* – you know.

JUDITH: I know. We've known since the middle of the nineteenth century.

SEBASTIAN: I haven't. I've only known for a couple of minutes.

JUDITH: Evolution.

(SEBASTIAN looks at her.)

The origin of the species. Evolution.

(SEBASTIAN looks at her.)

It's called evolution. What you're describing. There's an established term for it: evolution.

SEBASTIAN: Big words, is that it? It's called revolution.

JUDITH: Oh well. Never mind. My grandfather wasn't a monkey.

SEBASTIAN: Frustrating. You're so frustrating.

JUDITH: Maybe if you have another shower you'll come up with something new. I mean, something really new.

SEBASTIAN: *(Depressed.)* Pff.

JUDITH: Or you could put something on? You're displaying behavioural problems.

(SEBASTIAN fetches his clothes and puts them on during the following.)

SEBASTIAN: We used to have fur all over our bodies, but then that stopped being sexy during reproduction and then – anyway. Talking about reproduction: where's Robert?

JUDITH: Isn't he in his room?

SEBASTIAN: *(Shouts.)* Robert?

(Nothing.)

He should be back by now.

JUDITH: Maybe he's still at judo.

SEBASTIAN: At this time?

JUDITH: *(Thinks of something.)* You know what, I think he had a competition today.

SEBASTIAN: Was that today?

JUDITH: Maybe one of us should have gone to it.

SEBASTIAN: I thought it was this weekend?

JUDITH: Or at least picked him up.

SEBASTIAN: Let the au pair do it.

JUDITH: The au pair. She has a name.

SEBASTIAN: So?

JUDITH: You could try and remember it.

SEBASTIAN: Why? In a couple of months she'll be gone and I'll have to remember a new name.

JUDITH: Tell me. What's her name?

SEBASTIAN: No idea. What's her name?

JUDITH: Is this a joke?

SEBASTIAN: No. Tell me.

JUDITH: Have you really forgotten the name of our au pair girl?

SEBASTIAN: She's not a girl, she's a young woman.

JUDITH: You noticed that, did you.

SEBASTIAN: So what's her name?

JUDITH: Unbelievable. Think.

SEBASTIAN: Anna.

JUDITH: No.

SEBASTIAN: Nearly all women are called Anna.

JUDITH: Not this one.

SEBASTIAN: So, what's her name? You don't know either, do you.

JUDITH: Of course I know what our au pair is called.

SEBASTIAN: You have no idea.

JUDITH: She's a pretty girl with good manners who speaks fluent German –

SEBASTIAN: And is called? Well?

JUDITH: She's called – and she can cook, and not just pasta with tomato sauce.

(EVA enters as an au pair. ROBERT is holding her hand. He's a child of about eight. EVA is carrying a large sports bag.)

SEBASTIAN: Eva, where have you and the little one been all this time?

EVA: Good evening, Frau Eckels, good evening, Herr Eckels. How are you.

JUDITH: Good.

EVA: I am glad to hear it. I am well.

JUDITH: That's nice, why are you so late?

EVA: Oh, I am sorry.

JUDITH: Why, it was a why question.

EVA: Tonight the examination for the eight kyu, the hachi-kyu in white and yellow, took place at the sports and athletics association of Niederoberaubergtal.

SEBASTIAN: So, Robert? Where's your belt?

(ROBERT starts to cry.)

EVA: Robert was disqualified due to wilful misconduct.

JUDITH: What? Robert, what did you do?

(ROBERT cries.)

SEBASTIAN: What did he do?

JUDITH: *(Still appalled.)* Wilful misconduct!

EVA: Despite repeated warnings Robert Eckels' constant talking distracted his opponents as well as the referees and disrupted the fight.

JUDITH: Constant talking? The boy never says anything.

SEBASTIAN: Robert, say something.

JUDITH: Why does he never say anything?

EVA: *(To ROBERT.)* Come on Bobby, it's not that bad, come here.

(She hugs and comforts him. ROBERT sucks his thumb.)

JUDITH: He really seems to like her.

SEBASTIAN: That's normal, isn't it?

EVA: Pardon?

JUDITH: He really seems to like you.

EVA: He does, doesn't he?

JUDITH: Robert, don't you want to come and join me?

(ROBERT, sulking, shakes his head.)

SEBASTIAN: *(To JUDITH.)* He's that age when they cling to your apron strings.

JUDITH: Whose apron strings are you talking about?

EVA: You mustn't take it personally, he barely knows you.

JUDITH: You're exaggerating, I do see him now and then.

EVA: When did you last see him?

JUDITH: At breakfast? No?

EVA: And? What did he eat?

JUDITH: No idea. Oats?

EVA: He's not a horse.

JUDITH: Does that mean I'm a bad mother?

EVA: Whose mother?

JUDITH: Because I can't recite his breakfast ingredients correctly.

EVA: Ingredients.

JUDITH: What?

EVA: Ingredients. With an i. Ingredients.

SEBASTIAN: But he's grown tall, don't you think?

JUDITH: Since when?

SEBASTIAN: Since you last saw him. We're very proud, we put marks on the doorframe.

JUDITH: I'm just wondering: we used to do fine without au pairs, didn't we?

EVA: I'd never leave my child with an au pair.

JUDITH: Oh really? Is it bad for them?

EVA: You never know. She might be sitting at the edge of the playground and while my child falls off the monkey bars she's shooting drugs up her arm.

JUDITH: Would you do something like that?

EVA: I look after my child myself. You can't delegate the duties of motherhood. Otherwise one day I'll wake up and my child is grown up and I never even knew it.

SEBASTIAN: That's understandable, isn't it?

JUDITH: Sebastian, I can't even remember when we hired this au pair girl. Was there a job interview, or what happened?

SEBASTIAN: What does that even mean: 'au pair'?

JUDITH: She's so rude.

SEBASTIAN: But she looks cute.

EVA: 'Au-pair', that's French, it means 'mutual'.

JUDITH: So you think this person looks cute.

SEBASTIAN: Of course she does. Don't you think so?

(JUDITH shrugs.)

Look at her.

JUDITH: Sebastian, I know I'm being silly, but are you having an affair with our au pair?

EVA: I told you, we don't have an au pair.

JUDITH: Right. I certainly wouldn't have hired you.

EVA: Me? What for?

JUDITH: To look after the boy.

EVA: What boy?

JUDITH: This one, what's his name?

EVA: Are you trying to deflect from the fact that you're losing your mind?

SEBASTIAN: *(To JUDITH.)* Perhaps I could offer you a schnapps?

JUDITH: A schnapps?

SEBASTIAN: You seem upset.

JUDITH: Yes, because that boy – Sebastian, are you sure that's our boy?

EVA: I'll get you a schnapps.

(Does it.)

JUDITH: I really can't remember this boy.

SEBASTIAN: Maybe because he's grown so tall?

JUDITH: What's your name, little boy?

ROBERT: Parplürlpnerlpraul.

JUDITH: Sebastian, what's he saying?

(SEBASTIAN looks at her.)

ROBERT: *(Repeats in exactly the same way.)* Parplürlpnerlpraul.

JUDITH: Little boy, I can't understand you.

(To SEBASTIAN.) Can you make out what he's saying?

SEBASTIAN: Of course, he said: Parplürlpnerlpraul.

(EVA returns with a schnapps.)

EVA: I think the last time she saw him was New Year's Eve, when he was allowed outside for a minute to look at the fireworks.

JUDITH: *(Referring to the schnapps.)* What am I supposed to do with this?

EVA: Drink it.

(JUDITH looks at her.)

Drink it. Like this.

(She demonstrates, drinks the schnapps.)

SEBASTIAN: Robert, do you remember Judith Eckels?

(ROBERT, sulking, shakes his head.)

JUDITH: Oh well, it doesn't matter. He was still very young.

SEBASTIAN: *(To ROBERT.)* Now tell us. What happened at judo today?

(ROBERT grabs JUDITH and throws her on the ground with an expert judo throw.)

EVA: That was pretty good.

SEBASTIAN: I agree: I don't understand why they didn't give you the belt.

JUDITH: Excuse me?

EVA: I thought his technique was pretty sophisticated.

SEBASTIAN: It had a certain elegance. Here, Robert, you can have my belt.

(He takes off his belt and hands it to ROBERT. ROBERT beams.)

ROBERT: Really, Papa?

SEBASTIAN: We don't give a toss about the referees.

ROBERT: Thank you, Papa.

(He puts the belt on.)

SEBASTIAN: Now my trousers are slipping.

(EVA hugs him and holds onto his trousers.)

EVA: You're such a good father. I'll be your trouser braces.

(She gives him a lengthy kiss. JUDITH gets up and straightens her clothes.)

JUDITH: Well, I had a nice time.

(EVA and SEBASTIAN kiss.)

'Mutual' I understand.

(The kiss continues.)

I guess I'll get going then.

(Kiss.)

Bye.

(Kiss.)

I said 'bye'.

(Kiss.)

(To ROBERT.) Bye, you. Thingy.

ROBERT: We'll meet again.

JUDITH: Oh really?

(EVA and SEBASTIAN stop kissing and listen to ROBERT.)

ROBERT: No matter where you're hiding, in the concrete jungles of the cities or in the wide-open spaces of the savannah, I can feel you in my body, I can smell your fear.

JUDITH: That's nice. Everyone always comes back anyway.

(She leaves.)

EVA: I can smell it too.

SEBASTIAN: Yes. There's kind of a funny smell.

EVA: But apart from that it looks nice.

SEBASTIAN: Not as big as in the photos.

EVA: The plant wasn't in them either.

SEBASTIAN: *(To Robert.)* So, have you had a look around?

EVA: The child's room is upstairs, that's what it said in the description.

ROBERT: I want to go skiing.

SEBASTIAN: Tomorrow. It's too late today.

ROBERT: But I want to go skiing now.

EVA: The ski lift is already closed.

SEBASTIAN: See, it's too dark as well.

EVA: Come on, let's go and look for the bath.

ROBERT: You always make the decisions.

SEBASTIAN: One day you'll have children of your own and then you can make the decisions.

ROBERT: One day, one day. It's always one day or tomorrow. I want it now.

EVA: Now there's only the bath. Come on.

ROBERT: For weeks you've talked of nothing else: we're going skiing, you have to sleep five more times then we'll go skiing, do your homework, then we'll go to Niederoberaubergtal and go skiing, and now we're here, and what's happening? Nothing. Boring bath. It's all a scam, it's all bullshit.

EVA: That's enough now.

ROBERT: It's nowhere near enough. It's lame. Really lame. You always make the rules. As if I was your slave.

EVA: You're making me cry.

SEBASTIAN: Stop it. You're going to do what your mother tells you. No backtalk.

ROBERT: You're such Nazis.

EVA: Such what?

ROBERT: Nazis. I want to go skiing.

SEBASTIAN: *(Raises a finger.)* O, o, o. That's no joking matter.

ROBERT: Nazi parents.

EVA: Who would say such a thing?

ROBERT: Me. Nazis. You've erected a totalitarian regime to suppress me.

EVA: Off to bed. That really is enough.

ROBERT: Yes, mein Führer.

(Hitler salute.)

EVA: No bath for you then.

(ROBERT has a tantrum, she pulls him outside.)

ROBERT: *(Protesting.)* Nazi-crap-fuck-fascist-Nazi-crap-parents.

(Screams offstage.) Skiing!

SEBASTIAN: *(To the audience.)* Well, I'm sorry about this, about this ugly scene. Of course you're thinking: what went wrong there, where did that come from, why is this child acting like this, and it's boring anyway: generational conflict, we've seen it thousands of times, and suddenly it's happening in your own family. You wouldn't believe what a cute baby he was, embarrassing, really embarrassing –

(EVA returns.)

EVA: What are you doing?

SEBASTIAN: I'm disowning our child. Robert is a disgrace.

EVA: Who are you talking to?

SEBASTIAN: I thought, harsh words were spoken, I should apologise.

EVA: Are you doing a monologue?

SEBASTIAN: I wouldn't call it a monologue.

EVA: We agreed not to do any more monologues.

SEBASTIAN: It was just a small one. Short one.

EVA: We're not talking to third parties. Just imagine there's a wall here. Okay? This is closed. You don't want to stand in a room by yourself and talk to the wall, do you?

SEBASTIAN: No.

EVA: That would be maladjusted. And you don't want that, do you?

SEBASTIAN: No, of course not.

EVA: Good. I'm glad we've got that sorted.

SEBASTIAN: Completely sorted.

EVA: Then I'll go back upstairs and wash our son.

SEBASTIAN: You do that.

EVA: And you're in control?

SEBASTIAN: In complete control.

EVA: Sooner or later the door's going to open and someone's going to come in who you can talk to. So far that's always been the case. That's why they put the door there.

SEBASTIAN: Don't worry.

EVA: Okay, darling.

(She leaves. SEBASTIAN stands around. Flicks the light off and then on again. He points at the fourth wall.)

SEBASTIAN: *(Says.)* Wall.

(He looks at the door and waits.)

I could sing a song.

(Sings a song. The door opens and JUDITH enters.)

JUDITH: Good evening.

SEBASTIAN: Good evening.

JUDITH: You found it all right?

SEBASTIAN: Yes, thank you.

JUDITH: Did you have a good journey?

SEBASTIAN: Everything was fine.

JUDITH: And this? You're happy with everything?

SEBASTIAN: We only just got here, but so far everything's fine.

JUDITH: That's what we like to hear. No complaints.

SEBASTIAN: Exactly. It smells a bit funny when you come in.

JUDITH: You mean it stinks?

SEBASTIAN: If that's how you want to put it.

JUDITH: Like rotting carcasses?

(SEBASTIAN looks at her.)

Decay?

SEBASTIAN: Decay?

JUDITH: *(Nods.)* All right. But apart from that?

SEBASTIAN: Apart from that?

JUDITH: Other than that.

SEBASTIAN: Nothing. I don't know why I'm so nervous.

JUDITH: You found the child's room.

SEBASTIAN: Yes. Upstairs.

JUDITH: The bathroom?

SEBASTIAN: Upstairs as well, apparently.

JUDITH: Good. I just wanted to check. Make sure everything is all right.

SEBASTIAN: Yes, thank you, everything is – exactly – that.

JUDITH: What?

SEBASTIAN: All right. Like you said.

JUDITH: Did I say that?

SEBASTIAN: Everything is all right.

(Nothing.)

JUDITH: Is everything all right?

SEBASTIAN: Everything is all right. A touch of nerves, but apart from that: ski heil!

JUDITH: Pardon?

SEBASTIAN: Ski heil. I don't know why you said that.

JUDITH: Me?

(SEBASTIAN looks at her.)

I said that?

SEBASTIAN: Yes, you: ski heil! That's what you said. No? What? I. Exactly. Me. I said that.

JUDITH: Are you sure everything is all right?

SEBASTIAN: Sure, sure.

(Nothing.)

JUDITH: You found the bed linen?

SEBASTIAN: My wife –

(SEBASTIAN looks at her.)

JUDITH: What about your wife?

SEBASTIAN: The bed linen – my wife – I think I'm going to be sick.

JUDITH: The toilet –

SEBASTIAN: No, I'm all right.

JUDITH: Good. I just wanted to check everything was all right.

SEBASTIAN: All right.

JUDITH: Yes. Right. Left. Right. But everything seems fine.

SEBASTIAN: Left. What I'd really like to know is –

JUDITH: Yes?

SEBASTIAN: What's in the parcel?

JUDITH: What parcel?

SEBASTIAN: There's a parcel on the table. There.

JUDITH: Did you have a look inside?

SEBASTIAN: Not yet.

JUDITH: Then of course you can't know what's inside.

SEBASTIAN: No.

JUDITH: And neither can I.

SEBASTIAN: No.

JUDITH: We don't know what's inside.

SEBASTIAN: No. Oh my God, we don't know.

JUDITH: Take it off.

SEBASTIAN: What?

JUDITH: The table. Just take it off the table.

(EVA enters. She's holding an ugly decorative dagger.)

EVA: I think there's something terribly wrong here.

JUDITH: Good evening.

EVA: Is it you?

JUDITH: What?

EVA: Is this your holiday flat?

SEBASTIAN: Eva, why are you being so rude?

EVA: This flat stinks.

SEBASTIAN: Well, then you can open the window for a bit.

EVA: The flat stinks from the inside, it's rotten to the core.

JUDITH: Is there something you're not happy with?

EVA: *(Referring to the dagger.)* What's this?

JUDITH: It's an ornamental piece.

EVA: Ornamental piece.

JUDITH: Yes, one of those things you hang on the wall so the flat looks more cosy.

EVA: There's a very cosy swastika on it.

JUDITH: Oh really?

EVA: Yes. Here, take a look.

(JUDITH looks.)

JUDITH: Well I never. I didn't realise.

EVA: Oh really. This is a Nazi dagger.

JUDITH: We-ell, we-ell.

EVA: Stop the we-elling, why is this hanging on your wall?

JUDITH: Just because there's a swastika on it doesn't mean it's a Nazi dagger.

EVA: And what else would it be?

JUDITH: The swastika is the Hindu sign of the sun.

EVA: But it doesn't look remotely Asian.

JUDITH: It's a symbol of luck, there's no reason to get hysterical.

EVA: This is exactly the kind of crap they gave the SS-people as a reward.

JUDITH: You really know a lot about this stuff, I suppose you're active yourself.

EVA: Sebastian, I don't want to stay with Nazis.

SEBASTIAN: It didn't say anything about this in the description. It said 'a pleasant atmosphere', not Nazi doss house.

JUDITH: You're getting yourself worked up.

SEBASTIAN: If you ask me you should mention that kind of thing. Then one can react accordingly.

JUDITH: Why does everything always have to be 'Nazi', it's such a tiny little knife.

(ROBERT enters dressed in a Nazi uniform.)

ROBERT: Heil Hitler.

EVA: Robert!

ROBERT: It was in the wardrobe with the sign that said 'private'.

JUDITH: We had a written agreement that this wardrobe wouldn't be opened.

EVA: Well? Is this a Hindu sun uniform?

(To ROBERT.) Robert, take that off at once.

ROBERT: I think it really suits me.

EVA: Sebastian, we're packing our things and then we're leaving. At once.

SEBASTIAN: We haven't even unpacked yet.

EVA: *(To ROBERT.)* I said the pyjamas, not the SS uniform, the pyjamas. I put the pyjamas out for you.

JUDITH: I commend the dashing appearance of our young comrade, but since our wardrobe was forcefully opened and our private property violated, I consider our rental agreement invalid.

EVA: Ah, so that's how you want to play it?

JUDITH: That's how I'm playing it.

EVA: You want to terminate our contract?

JUDITH: Throw you out, as it were.

EVA: We're not staying here anyway.

JUDITH: Without notice. Kick you out.

EVA: I'm not staying under this roof for a second longer. Sebastian, come on.

JUDITH: Effective immediately.

EVA: Do you know what you are?

JUDITH: Me? No idea, I have no idea what I am, please, my gracious lady, do enlighten me.

EVA: You're a Nazi slut, and I, I'm –

JUDITH: Yes, you, what about you?

EVA: I'm going to have you put you behind bars.

JUDITH: Behind bars.

EVA: Exactly. Behind bars.

JUDITH: Out! You're fired.

EVA: Fired. That's ridiculous. Nazi slut!

JUDITH: Why don't you go back to where you came from. We don't need you here. We didn't invite you. Open your wardrobes at home if you have any, you starvelings. And so on.

SEBASTIAN: I'll be in touch about the deposit.

EVA: Sebastian, are you coming?

(They leave.)

ROBERT: May I?

(Takes the dagger, tries to attach it to his uniform.)

How did this work again?

JUDITH: I think it's a bit much.

ROBERT: Wasn't my idea.

JUDITH: I didn't tell you to dress up as a Nazi officer.

ROBERT: *(Concerned.)* You think it doesn't suit me?

JUDITH: I don't know. Raises funny associations.

ROBERT: Unpleasant associations?

JUDITH: Well. You look like a Nazi.

ROBERT: But it's just a costume.

JUDITH: Yes, but will people understand that?

ROBERT: When are they coming anyway?

JUDITH: Any moment.

ROBERT: And you?

JUDITH: Me?

ROBERT: What are you dressed as?

JUDITH: Jesus, Christ Almighty, I completely forgot.

ROBERT: Nordic nights.

(Referring to her skirt.) Are those pleats meant to be the aurora borealis?

JUDITH: What am I going to do?

ROBERT: Nordic nights. I'm not the one who came up with it.

JUDITH: I'll have to improvise.

(She hurries offstage to change.)

ROBERT: And you think they're going to find my costume upsetting?

JUDITH: *(From offstage.)* It's just a bit obvious.

ROBERT: Obvious how?

JUDITH: *(From offstage.)* Nazi. There's not much room for interpretation.

ROBERT: Interpretation?

JUDITH: *(From offstage.)* Yes. You should leave an interactive space so people can have their own associations. With the way you're dressed –

ROBERT: Yes?

JUDITH: *(From offstage.)* Well, you come in and everyone immediately knows, Robert is a Nazi.

ROBERT: I don't want our guests to think, hmm, is he dressed as a Nazi or could that be an Indian.

JUDITH: *(From offstage.)* I'm just saying. Your costume isn't exactly dazzlingly ambivalent.

ROBERT: You'd prefer me to look dazzlingly ambivalent?

JUDITH: *(From offstage.)* Not quite as obvious anyway.

ROBERT: Nordic nights. That's bullshit. Why Nordic nights? Brazilian nights would have been a lot sexier.

JUDITH: *(From offstage.)* And you could have kept the costume.

(JUDITH re-enters. She's dressed as a Viking from head to toe, down to the last detail, including a helmet with horns, a blonde wig with braids, a fur doublet and a club.)

ROBERT: I see, so you had to improvise.

JUDITH: Whatever I could come up with at such short notice.

ROBERT: So that's dazzlingly ambivalent, is it?

JUDITH: This is just something I've quickly thrown together.

ROBERT: Nothing too obvious.

JUDITH: I'd like it if you could change, too.

ROBERT: Into something like this, where you have something to puzzle over, what could she be, that costume, is she a cowboy or a pirate? Something along those lines, yes?

JUDITH: I'd like that, yes, so people won't think I'm married to a Nazi –

(The doorbell rings.)

ROBERT: Fine. I'll just have to improvise, then. Nordic nights.

JUDITH: Yes, please. Thank you.

(ROBERT leaves. JUDITH opens the door for SEBASTIAN and EVA. SEBASTIAN is dressed as an elk. EVA is a volcano, a crown as an eruption, a cloak as a grey mountain with lava running down it.)

JUDITH: Aah! Ooh! A stag and a, er, thingy.

SEBASTIAN: Elk.

JUDITH: *(Referring to EVA.)* This? That doesn't look like an elk.

SEBASTIAN: Me. I'm the elk.

JUDITH: Oh really?

SEBASTIAN: Not a stag. Elk. I'm an elk.

JUDITH: Aah. An elk. You're an elk. Nordic nights, Scandinavia, I get it. Elk.

(To EVA.) And you?

SEBASTIAN: *(To EVA.)* You see?

EVA: What?

SEBASTIAN: You can't tell what you're dressed as.

EVA: Of course you can tell.

SEBASTIAN: She just asked you, she can't tell.

EVA: Yeah, right.

SEBASTIAN: *(To JUDITH.)* Can you tell what this is?

JUDITH: To be honest –

SEBASTIAN: She can't tell, you see?

EVA: *(To JUDITH.)* You know what I am.

(JUDITH looks at her.)

Come on Judith, don't play dumb.

JUDITH: I'm not playing dumb, it's just that –

SEBASTIAN: She can't tell, she's not playing dumb, it's just completely unclear what you're supposed to be.

(A clattering sound. ROBERT enters. He's dressed as a skier: a scarf, a bobble cap or helmet, ski goggles, thick mittens, long skis on his shoulder, heavy ski boots on his feet.)

JUDITH: What's up with you?

ROBERT: Nordic nights.

SEBASTIAN: You. Are. A. Skier? A skier. Look Eva, that's completely clear. Robert is a skier. Are you a skier, Robert?

ROBERT: I'm a skier, and you're a stag.

SEBASTIAN: Elk.

ROBERT: Elk. Of course. Elk. Scandinavia.

JUDITH: And I'm a Viking.

SEBASTIAN: *(To EVA, as if she's retarded.)* She's a Viking. Nordic nights: Viking.

ROBERT: *(To EVA.)* And you, you're – what are you?

SEBASTIAN: *(To EVA.)* You see?

EVA: Robert, stop fooling around, what am I?

ROBERT: Hello, Eva. You're –

EVA: Yes?

ROBERT: You're –

(To JUDITH.) Is that the kind of thing you meant when you said dazzlingly ambivalent?

EVA: I'm what?

JUDITH: No, there should be room for association.

SEBASTIAN: You see, Eva, there's no room for association.

EVA: Robert?

ROBERT: Yes, Eva.

EVA: What am I?

ROBERT: *(Uncertain.)* The snow queen?

(To SEBASTIAN.) Is she the snow queen?

JUDITH: She doesn't look like a snow queen.

ROBERT: No idea, have you ever seen one, a snow queen I mean, what do they look like?

JUDITH: You're the one that said snow queen not me, but I guess they're white, with snow and stuff.

ROBERT: To be honest I don't actually know what that is: a snow queen.

JUDITH: Not something like that.

SEBASTIAN: You hear the nonsense they're talking? Snow queen. No one knows what you're supposed to be.

ROBERT: What is she supposed to be?

EVA: *(Has a tantrum.)* Are you stupid, all of you? A blind person could work it out. I'm a volcano. I'm erupting. My head is exploding, this is blistering magma flying out of me, these are streams of liquid lava, there's an enormous smoke cloud rising from my crater, the earth is trembling and for several days a thick rain of ash will cover everything and nothing will grow here for decades.

ROBERT: Radioactive, eh?

SEBASTIAN: Crater? What crater?

JUDITH: Volcano?

EVA: Of course, obviously, a volcano. Lava, ash, debris. Like I said, a volcano.

JUDITH: And what does that have to do with Nordic nights?

SEBASTIAN: That's what I said: Etna, that's Italy, Vesuvius, Pompeii, that's all Italy, Krakatoa, Indonesia, that's all in the South. Southern nights, eh?

EVA: Snæffelsjökull.

(The others look at her.)

EVA: *(Repeats.)* Snæffelsjökull.

SEBASTIAN: Eva, why do you keep saying Snæffelsjökull?

EVA: That's Iceland. The North. It's a volcano in Iceland. Okay? Am I allowed to stay?

ROBERT: Yes, sure, Snæffel, stay, please stay.

JUDITH: Drinks anyone?

SEBASTIAN: You just made that up, this Snæffelcrap.

EVA: Snæffelsjökull, it's not my fault you're geographically challenged.

SEBASTIAN: *(To JUDITH and ROBERT.)* Have you heard of this Snæffelthingy?

EVA: Jökull, Snæffelsjökull. What, do you want me to leave? Is that what you want? Shall I leave?

SEBASTIAN: All right, all right, I like your imagination-

ROBERT: Let's dance.

(He puts on some music.)

EVA: Do you have an atlas?

SEBASTIAN: I can't dance.

JUDITH: Robert always wants to dance. There's four of us, Robert, this is not a disco.

ROBERT: Who cares. Let's dance.

(He grabs EVA and dances with her.)

JUDITH: He's just doing this to humiliate me. I can't dance.

ROBERT: She can't dance, but who cares. *I* can dance.

SEBASTIAN: Well – I definitely can't.

EVA: *(To SEBASTIAN.)* Come on and dance, darling, dance.

ROBERT: Everyone can dance.

SEBASTIAN: I can't.

JUDITH: *(Sarcastic.)* Look at the way they're moving, it's so sensual. Robert has rhythm in his blood.

EVA: He really is a good dancer. Robert, I love the way you dance.

SEBASTIAN: *(Copies her.)* Robert, I love the way you dance, blah blah blah.

ROBERT: Come on, Judith, don't be a goat.

JUDITH: Did he just call me a goat?

(JUDITH grabs SEBASTIAN and dances with strained abandon.)

SEBASTIAN: I – I can't dance.

JUDITH: Never mind, let's do it.

(They dance.)

SEBASTIAN: I'm very unhappy.

JUDITH: You really can't dance, can you.

(ROBERT and EVA laugh sarcastically.)

Don't jiggle so much.

SEBASTIAN: But that's what the music is like.

JUDITH: Forget the music. Just hold on.

SEBASTIAN: Like this?

JUDITH: Wrap yourself around me. We're doing the blues.

SEBASTIAN: But isn't this actually an up-tempo foxtrot?

JUDITH: Put your cheek against my cheek and feel the heat.

(SEBASTIAN tries it.)

Do you feel it?

SEBASTIAN: *(Surprised.)* Hmm. Nice and warm.

EVA: What are they doing?

ROBERT: Judith.

(JUDITH, in a daze, dances with SEBASTIAN, in a daze. Cheek to cheek.)

ROBERT: Judith, you're doing the blues.

(To EVA.) They're doing the blues.

(To JUDITH.) Judith, this is an up-tempo foxtrot. You can do the disco fox to it if you want. Or the cha cha cha or the jive. But not the blues. This bears no resemblance to dancing. This is – you're – playing hide the salami, that's all.

JUDITH: *(Keeps dancing.)* Did you say something, darling?

ROBERT: Do we have to call each other darling just because we're having an argument?

JUDITH: I'm not having an argument, I'm dancing.

EVA: Sebastian, what are you doing?

SEBASTIAN: *(As if he's waking up.)* Hmm?

JUDITH: This feels a bit edgy and tense.

(JUDITH and SEBASTIAN stop dancing.)

Shall we all have a cocktail and loosen up?

ROBERT: You're not having a cocktail and you're definitely not loosening up.

SEBASTIAN: *(To JUDITH.)* Can I give you a hand with the mixing?

EVA: Why are you saying it like that?

JUDITH: *(On her way to the kitchen.)* Watch out, you slinky elk, I'm a merciless hunter and I'm carrying a club.

SEBASTIAN: I always carry my club as well.

(They disappear into the kitchen.)

EVA: Did you hear that, Robert?

(ROBERT turns off the music.)

ROBERT: *(Bitter.)* I suppose it was inevitable: one couple invites another couple and then it's like a law of nature, you're frustrated in general and then partner A sleeps with the partner of partner B, and then partner B is upset and in order to punish them he sleeps with the partner of partner A, and then for a while everyone thinks they're breaking out of the constraints of their bourgeois marriage, but then they realise that it doesn't really make them any more free but that this, too, is a well-trodden bourgeois pattern of escape and that somehow they all feel small, lonely and gross, unpleasantly hungover somehow, and that's also because in order to manage even this rudimentary crossing of boundaries they had to pour copious amounts of alcohol down their throats to numb their overly-stimulated superegos, and there they are, sitting there, or rather crawling there literally with their tails between their legs, crawling back to their depressing relationships in order to wait for the next half-hearted attempt to escape legitimised by ridiculous costumes.

(Nothing.)

EVA: Hmm.

ROBERT: Isn't that right.

EVA: Yes.

ROBERT: Exactly.

(Nothing.)

EVA: And?

ROBERT: What?

EVA: Does that mean we have to – ?

ROBERT: You mean because it's inevitable anyway?

EVA: It is. Isn't it?

ROBERT: In that case, let's –

(They grope each other. Uninspired.)

EVA: Why are your hands so hot? Are they wet?

ROBERT: I don't know. Metabolism.

EVA: You have a metabolism?

ROBERT: Yes, it's really bad.

(They attempt a kiss. JUDITH and SEBASTIAN enter with cocktails.)

SEBASTIAN: We have cocktails. Oh.

JUDITH: Aha. You've progressed.

(To EVA.) And, how's he doing?

SEBASTIAN: Eh? I don't get it.

JUDITH: Is something wrong? It makes perfect sense: the skier mounts the volcano.

SEBASTIAN: Eva, why are you doing this? You always said Robert was a piffling trifle.

ROBERT: A piffling trifle?

EVA: Yes, don't be upset, I did say that.

ROBERT: A piffling trifle. What's that supposed to mean, a piffling trifle?

EVA: Negligible.

ROBERT: Negligible.

EVA: Yes, don't be offended. In my world you were just more of a random figure.

ROBERT: A random figure.

EVA: Yes, something that's kind of on the periphery.

ROBERT: The periphery.

EVA: Up to now you weren't the lead, you were more of a supporting role, up to now.

ROBERT: A supporting role, I see.

SEBASTIAN: Up to now? But now your world suddenly looks completely different because his skis are so long, suddenly he's the eponymous hero in your world, or what, eh?

JUDITH: It was clear that when the two of us went into the kitchen they would loosen up in here. It happens in every four-character play: sexual intercourse with partner-swapping and subsequent depression.

SEBASTIAN: Partner swapping, aha. Does that mean we should just join them and have a grope as well?

JUDITH: *(Asks the other two.)* How far did you get?

EVA: Well, the beginning of the middle bit, right?

ROBERT: Yes, I'd agree: the beginning of the middle bit, round there, kind of.

JUDITH: I just meant, is it still worth us joining in?

ROBERT: The two of you?

JUDITH: Yes, since you've been at it for a while, and so far we've just been mixing.

ROBERT: Mixing?

JUDITH: Yes.

ROBERT: *(Truly shocked.)* You've been mixing?

SEBASTIAN: Mixing. The cocktails.

EVA: *(To Robert.)* Or shall we have a cocktail first? I mean – only if you don't mind.

ROBERT: Oh, nono, no problem, let's just drink our cocktails, I wasn't really in the –

EVA: No, me neither.

JUDITH: *(Referring to the cocktails.)* Here, we've got four Elephant Nose Blows.

EVA: Elephant what?

JUDITH: Nose Blows: curaçao, ginger ale, vodka, cranberry, lime juice, cane sugar and crispy bacon. Elephant Nose Blow.

EVA: Aha. Sounds yummy.

(Everyone sits down and takes a cocktail.)

JUDITH: Prost.

ROBERT: Exactly.

(They clink glasses.)

SEBASTIAN: *(Nods admiringly, referring to the cocktail.)* Hmm.

EVA: Go for it.

JUDITH: Hmm.

ROBERT: It's all right.

(Nothing.)

SEBASTIAN: What's in the parcel?

JUDITH: No idea. Have you had a look, Robert?

ROBERT: No. The parcel is still closed. No one's had a look.

EVA: Don't you want to open it?

JUDITH: No.

ROBERT: No. Not really.

SEBASTIAN: I see.

(Nothing.)

JUDITH: So, Robert here is seeking new career opportunities.

ROBERT: Judith, don't.

JUDITH: Why not, it's not a secret.

SEBASTIAN: *(Completely shocked.)* Robert! Is that true?

ROBERT: Well. Yes. I thought, after ten years of going down the beaten track.

EVA: But you love your job.

ROBERT: Well. Yes. No.

EVA: You were always so happy.

ROBERT: Not really. I just said that so you'd leave me alone.

SEBASTIAN: You've been fired.

ROBERT: Nono. I just thought, I'm pushing forty, what have I achieved?

SEBASTIAN: Yeah, right. You've been fired.

ROBERT: There's misery, hunger, war wherever you look.

EVA: But not because of you.

JUDITH: I think it's nice that he thinks like that.

ROBERT: And every day I get up at seven and go to the office.

SEBASTIAN: Yes, but, Robert –

ROBERT: Hmm?

SEBASTIAN: If you don't go to the office that doesn't change anything.

ROBERT: Listen. The important thing is that I'm taking control.

SEBASTIAN: And then?

ROBERT: What do you mean and then?

EVA: What are you going to do instead?

ROBERT: Oh. I don't know. Something different.

JUDITH: Robert would like to do something with wood.

(Nothing.)

SEBASTIAN: With wood?

(ROBERT nods, embarrassed.)

ROBERT: That's right. I'd like to do something with wood.

(Nothing.)

SEBASTIAN: Wood.

EVA: Well. Never mind.

SEBASTIAN: I always thought you wanted to do something with people.

ROBERT: No. Not any more. Not really.

SEBASTIAN: Okay. Wood.

(Nothing.)

I don't think it's that bad that they've fired you, these things happen, some people get fired, others don't. *(Nothing. SEBASTIAN's cocktail is finished, he makes slurping sounds with his straw.)*

EVA: Sebastian.

SEBASTIAN: *(Keeps slurping.)* Hmm?

EVA: Stop it.

SEBASTIAN: What?

(He slurps.)

EVA: It sounds like snot.

SEBASTIAN: It's not snot, it's cane sugar.

EVA: You've had enough cane sugar.

(She takes his glass, SEBASTIAN keeps the straw in his mouth. EVA carries SEBASTIAN's glass and her own into the kitchen.)

EVA: Top-up?

JUDITH: I'll have another one, you too, Robert?

ROBERT: Thanks, I still have some.

(JUDITH takes his glass anyway, follows EVA into the kitchen.)

Hey, I still have some.

SEBASTIAN: *(Shrugs.)* Women.

ROBERT: What?

SEBASTIAN: I said: women. That's what they're like. They take your cocktail while you're still drinking.

ROBERT: No, Sebastian, that's not what women are like, I don't like this kind of thing, this we're-all-mates-type bonding where the men chink beer bottles and agree that the women are stupid. Women aren't stupid.

SEBASTIAN: But have you never – ?

ROBERT: What?

SEBASTIAN: Have you never felt like – ?

ROBERT: Felt like what?

SEBASTIAN: Come on, Robert, drop the fresh-out-of-the-convent act.

ROBERT: I'm not – what do you mean convent?

SEBASTIAN: You know, one of those convents. Full of monks, young men, with barely any fluff in their armpits.

ROBERT: What?!

SEBASTIAN: Relax.

ROBERT: At the moment I'm not feeling even remotely relaxed.

SEBASTIAN: They're in the kitchen and the Elephant Nose Blow takes a while.

ROBERT: What does that have to do with it?

SEBASTIAN: With what?

ROBERT: With your friars.

SEBASTIAN: You see, you've thought about it as well.

ROBERT: Me?!

SEBASTIAN: You lift up their frocks and there's a huge, throbbing club, hmm, Robert?

ROBERT: Is this because of your elk costume or are you completely losing your mind?

SEBASTIAN: I'm completely losing my mind. Your thick, heavy ski boots are driving me crazy.

ROBERT: Stay there.

SEBASTIAN: Come on, Robert, you want it too.

ROBERT: Me? Definitely not. Stay there. I'm going to scream.

SEBASTIAN: I like the fact that you're so sensitive. It turns me on.

ROBERT: But I don't want you to get turned on, I'd rather you kept acting normal and slept with my wife.

SEBASTIAN: Forget about your wife. Give yourself to the elk.

ROBERT: Pardon?

SEBASTIAN: Give yourself to the elk.

ROBERT: Can you hear yourself? You sound like a Swedish advertising brochure.

SEBASTIAN: Who gives a fuck, give yourself to him.

ROBERT: No.

SEBASTIAN: To the elk.

ROBERT: I'd rather not, please.

SEBASTIAN: You have no idea what you want.

ROBERT: Yes I do.

SEBASTIAN: What you really want.

ROBERT: Yes I do, I'd like to do something with wood.

SEBASTIAN: What you really, truly want. Deep inside you.

ROBERT: Deep inside me the Elephant Nose Blow is rumbling around, that's it.

SEBASTIAN: Deep inside, you want me.

ROBERT: You? Of all people?

SEBASTIAN: You see.

(He touches him.)

ROBERT: Sebastian, you're a nice guy –

SEBASTIAN: I'm not nice, I'm an elk.

(He attacks him. ROBERT fights back.)

ROBERT: *(Suddenly aggressive.)* All right then, come here, I'll have you for breakfast, you little weed.

SEBASTIAN: Then take me, Robert, take me.

(An intense wrestling match, it becomes passionate and finally sexual from both sides. EVA enters, during the following she carries the potted plant into the kitchen. She continues her conversation with JUDITH in the kitchen without paying any attention to SEBASTIAN and ROBERT.)

EVA: *(Gabbling away.)* – and I said to Sebastian, I have no idea where this parcel came from. I didn't put it there, and then he said: does it say who sent it, and I had a look, and would you believe, it says my name, that I sent it, and I thought, the cheek, who would send parcels in my name, and I went to have a closer look and then I saw that it looked exactly like my handwriting –

JUDITH: *(Calls from the kitchen.)* So what was in the parcel?

EVA: I'll be right there.

(To SEBASTIAN and ROBERT, who are oblivious to her and still sexually active.) Don't let me disturb you, I'm just getting this funny plant.

(Carries the plant into the kitchen. As she's leaving.)

So it was exactly like my handwriting, and that did make me wonder, my handwriting isn't that easy to imitate, I'm very special, it very distinctly expresses my personality, and my personality is extremely unusual, I'm sort of the only one that has it, it's like it was made to measure –

(She's gone without having clocked ROBERT and SEBASTIAN's activities. The two of them sink onto the couch, exhausted.)

SEBASTIAN: And? Was that so bad?

ROBERT: I'm speechless.

SEBASTIAN: It's always like that the first time. I was embarrassed at first as well.

ROBERT: I'm not embarrassed. It's just that I had no idea such feelings even existed.

SEBASTIAN: What kind of feelings?

ROBERT: Sebastian. I'm overwhelmed. I've just slept with an elk.

SEBASTIAN: And, wasn't it good?

ROBERT: I don't know what I've been doing all these years. What a waste. From now on, this is what I want.

SEBASTIAN: Aha?

ROBERT: Only elks.

SEBASTIAN: But you do realise –

ROBERT: What?

SEBASTIAN: That that was me.

ROBERT: Yes. You're my elk.

SEBASTIAN: Yes, sure, but –

ROBERT: I'm going to leave Judith, we'll move to a little cottage, you and me, up in Lapland, I'll go fishing and you'll stand next to me and graze by the lush lake shore.

SEBASTIAN: Robert, I don't want to rob you of your illusions –

ROBERT: What do elks eat? Do they gnaw the bark off the trees?

SEBASTIAN: Pork belly.

ROBERT: Pork belly?

SEBASTIAN: Pork belly is my favourite. Three or four slices, fried in a pan, and mashed potatoes on the side.

ROBERT: Oh really? I thought vegetarian, but who cares, as long as I have my furry elk.

SEBASTIAN: Robert, this is making me unhappy.

ROBERT: What, sweetie?

SEBASTIAN: I feel like all you care about is the elk.

ROBERT: Of course. What else would I care about?

SEBASTIAN: What about me?

ROBERT: I don't get it.

SEBASTIAN: I can tell you're fixated on my antlers and not on me as a person.

ROBERT: Oh dearie me, here we go. Do you really need inner values as well, mousie? What do you want to be, a demi-god? You're an animal and you've just awakened my sexuality, isn't that enough. If you want me to fall in love with your insides as well that's asking too much, really, mousie.

SEBASTIAN: But it's just a costume.

ROBERT: It doesn't matter, you put it on and everything's peachy.

SEBASTIAN: But then you can't see me, what I'm like, as a person.

ROBERT: I can see what you're like as an elk.

SEBASTIAN: I'm not sure that's enough for me in the long run.

(JUDITH and EVA return.)

JUDITH: Four Elephant Nose Blows.

EVA: So, was it very boring without us?

SEBASTIAN: Eva, I missed you so.

ROBERT: Haha, that's good.

JUDITH: Robert, don't be mean.

ROBERT: It's just that he said he missed her.

JUDITH: Leave him alone if he wants to inject some romance into his relationship.

ROBERT: Judith, I'm leaving you.

JUDITH: Oh really?

ROBERT: Sebastian and I are going to live by a fjord.

EVA: With Sebastian?

ROBERT: We're a couple.

EVA: You're a couple.

ROBERT: A couple. Meaning lovers. Partners. A couple. Sebastian, explain it to her.

SEBASTIAN: There's nothing to explain.

ROBERT: Sebastian is playing it down a bit. It's a cut in both of our lives and at the same time a move to pastures new.

EVA: Sebastian, what's he on about?

SEBASTIAN: I have no idea, really. All we did was sit here and talk.

ROBERT: *(Solemnly.)* Judith, Eva: Sebastian and I, we made love.

JUDITH: You did what?

ROBERT: Made love. Love. On this sofa. And when I use this word, then I'm entirely aware of its all-encompassing meaning. The feeling I'm trying to describe is just as all-encompassing.

JUDITH: I guess nothing is off-limits tonight.

EVA: Sebastian, did you – again?

SEBASTIAN: Me? I've never – what makes you think that?

EVA: Unbelievable. Did you fuck Robert?

ROBERT: There was no fucking here, there was no shagging, there was no humping, for a few moments this modest living room became a temple in which the God of Love was worshipped. Venus, Amor, Cupid, you consecrated this place with your presence.

JUDITH: He's gone mad. Robert, you've gone mad. The cocktails were too much for him.

EVA: I'm afraid he's telling the truth. Sebastian, how could you? Robert is your best friend.

SEBASTIAN: But I didn't – what would I do with Robert? I mean: Robert! Sorry, but I'm not that desperate.

ROBERT: Excuse me?

SEBASTIAN: *(To ROBERT.)* Why are you giving the girls such a fright? I don't think that's right.

ROBERT: Sebastian, you can't deny –

SEBASTIAN: I deny, I deny. I deny everything. What he's saying is rubbish, all of it. Robert, you're drunk.

ROBERT: I'm not drunk, I'm speechless.

EVA: I'm speechless too, Sebastian.

ROBERT: *(To SEBASTIAN.)* I'm now going to take your hand and walk you through that door, into a new life. To Lapland.

SEBASTIAN: No.

ROBERT: Your hoof. Elks are cloven-hoofed animals.

JUDITH: He really can't handle his drink.

ROBERT: You're not taking me seriously. Sebastian. Why are you still sitting there? It was as beautiful for you as it was for me.

SEBASTIAN: *(Screams at him.)* That's enough, you pansy queen. Sit down and cut the adolescent gaggle or I'm going to clip you round the ears.

ROBERT: *(Starts to cry.)* Why are you doing this to me? Why?

EVA: Exactly. Why are you doing this to him?

ROBERT: *(To EVA.)* You keep out of it, dolly.

(To SEBASTIAN.) Sebastian. I opened up to you. I trusted you with my young, innocent body and you did all those wonderful things with it.

SEBASTIAN: Nope, rubbish, all of it.

ROBERT: Oh, that hurts. That really hurts.

JUDITH: Young and innocent! You must be off your rocker! You're pushing forty!

ROBERT: For the last time: Come. Come with me. Through this door and up North.

SEBASTIAN: Should we call a doctor?

ROBERT: If you don't come with me now you'll never see me again.

SEBASTIAN: Robert. Sit down. You're a mess.

(To JUDITH.) Does this happen a lot?

JUDITH: He can't handle it. Not cocktails, anyway.

ROBERT: *(To JUDITH.)* Hush your mouth.

(To SEBASTIAN.) Look at me. Look at me, Sebastian.

SEBASTIAN: Okay.

ROBERT: Did all of this mean nothing to you?

SEBASTIAN: All of what, I don't know what you're talking about.

ROBERT: Is that your final word?

SEBASTIAN: I mean – I'm sorry, but you're not playing with a full deck.

ROBERT: *(Nods.)* Adieu.

JUDITH: Robert. Have a sip of water.

ROBERT: *(Sobs.)* Adieu. Adieu.

(He leaves. No one knows what to do.)

SEBASTIAN: Well, er, I'd say he's lost the plot.

EVA: *(To JUDITH.)* Don't you want to go after him?

JUDITH: He'll be back. It's just a phase. You came back as well, didn't you.

EVA: We did?

JUDITH: Everyone always comes back. If not before, then as soon as the lights go off. Someone turns them back on and there they all are. And even if the last time we saw them they were crying and stabbing each other with a stupid knife, there they are, they clean themselves up, hold each other's hands and laugh. In my experience it's always like that.

SEBASTIAN: That's true. Maybe Robert's just gone to judo class.

EVA: Robert does judo?

JUDITH: Yes, I put him down for a course because he got beaten up once, on his way home.

EVA: Robert got beaten up?

SEBASTIAN: Yes, but today he's taking some kind of belt, what was it called again, my treasure?

JUDITH: Hachi-kyu, it's the eighth kyu in white and yellow.

EVA: Did you just call her my treasure?

SEBASTIAN: Other people pick animals and say mousie, bunny, little lamb or piggy, we prefer to be a bit more abstract because we're not really into animalistic stuff and use my treasure, all it means is that we're precious to each other.

EVA: You're precious to each other.

JUDITH: Some people think that the economic factor is a bit unromantic and prefer to act cosmopolitan and call each other cherie, liebling or, Mediterranean style, amore mio.

SEBASTIAN: Or they turn each other into pets and call each other beaver or pussy.

JUDITH: I think it's each to their own: chubby, booby, willie, mickey, stinky, smiley, pokey or whatever.

EVA: I'm sorry, I'm a bit confused.

SEBASTIAN: That's all right. You haven't been with us that long.

EVA: So you're having an intimate relationship and Robert got beaten up?

SEBASTIAN: Of course, Anna, but I'm sorry, I'm in a bit of a hurry.

EVA: Anna?

SEBASTIAN: Your name isn't Anna?

EVA: No!

SEBASTIAN: Nearly all women are called Anna.

EVA: I'm not, my name is Eva.

SEBASTIAN: Anyway, I'd be grateful if you got a move on.

EVA: What do you mean get a move on?

SEBASTIAN: Judith, help me out here, our Anna here doesn't understand anything.

EVA: Eva.

JUDITH: Well, Anna, the glasses go into the kitchen, in the dishwasher, but I'd rather start it myself, and then start by taking out the rubbish –

EVA: Dishwasher –

SEBASTIAN: Yes, that's what it's called.

EVA: The rubbish –

JUDITH: All this stuff lying around here.

EVA: I can do that, but I'm a guest here, right?

SEBASTIAN: A guest. Oh dear.

(To JUDITH.) Where did you find her?

JUDITH: *(To EVA.)* A little bit of clearing up, is that too much to ask? Are you so incredibly special?

(EVA looks at her.)

Anna? Lena? Charlotte? Parplürlpnerlpraul?

SEBASTIAN: She doesn't understand anything.

(Very aggressive, as if she's completely stupid.) I not pay for giving stupid looks, you cleaning slag.

EVA: It comes into my hearing and out the other side, because I am lacking in full comprehension, which doesn't understand it. But my innerpersonal homunculus ducks under the enormous volume erupting from this male pressure airtube, and in order to survive adapts to those most adapted to the adapted way of life.

(She starts to tidy up.)

SEBASTIAN: What's that?

EVA: Nothing, I'm merely cleaning up what's fallen down, because it falls from people and disappears under the furniture unless I kneel down, so I get it back from under the furniture, on shovels and brooms and knees, because that's what I'm here for.

(SEBASTIAN makes a dismissive gesture.)

SEBASTIAN: Whatever.

(To JUDITH.) I'm starting to get peckish.

JUDITH: Of course, darling, peckish.

(JUDITH goes into the kitchen.)

EVA: Critics of civilisation have vandalised their rubbish underneath this beaten-up sofa, now the rubbishknot has gotten stuck there and has to be opened by the good houseflymaid.

(She tries to reach the rubbish under the sofa.)

SEBASTIAN: Aren't there any German cleaning ladies left?

(JUDITH enters with a tin of apricot slices from the kitchen.)

JUDITH: We're short of almost everything now. These apricot slices for example are all we have left. After this all we can do is chew our fingernails.

SEBASTIAN: We'll be fine, we've always been fine. Isn't that right?

JUDITH: Be fine, that's correct. Does anyone have a tin opener?

EVA: Nothing at hand, no metal equipment for opening up, but to mouth, from hand to mouth, I have a toothed cog between my licking lips so I can bite open the tincan with the toothedcograilway, so I can get a little apricot slice between my teeth since I'm such a good houseflybusybee.

SEBASTIAN: Is she planning to bite it open?

JUDITH: If that's the only way.

(SEBASTIAN makes a dismissive gesture.)

SEBASTIAN: Whatever. She won't get any apricots anyway.

JUDITH: Shush.

SEBASTIAN: Because otherwise we won't have enough and we come first, I mean we're important, it's about us, she's just a cleaning woman and not even from around here.

JUDITH: Don't rub it in her face or she won't open the tin.

(To EVA.)

Be a good girl, cleaning lady, and open the little tin so you can have a nice slice of fruit.

EVA: And the little cleaner girl is cleaning strong and tears open the tin with the toothypegs in her head.

(She bites open the tin.)

SEBASTIAN: The things they're still able to do, these exotic species from abroad, my teeth would fall out one by one and tumble onto my lap.

EVA: And now in with the fingergrips into the soft juicesauce, because I'm a fruitflesh-eating cleaning plant.

SEBASTIAN: *(Headbutts her.)* Step away from the contents of the tin. It's mine.

(Grabs the tin.)

JUDITH: Go on and give her a piece.

SEBASTIAN: Nope.

(He stuffs his face.)

JUDITH: At least leave some for me. It's the last tin.

SEBASTIAN: Here, eat, woman, so you don't keel over.

(They eat from the tin.)

EVA: And the cleaning woman who toothed the tin shell open? What does she get?

SEBASTIAN: The cleaning lady can get a punch in the mouth if she really wants something in her mouth.

EVA: She's weakened-down and has made a little poetry so she may take part in the apri-delicacies:

Oh, so wery wery weak,
Watch me weep and weep,
Woe my weedy weakening weins,
Watch me,
Woe my warring will,
Woe a wallowing weakening whack.
Watch me:
Woe weeping willow.
What misery, weep, weep.

(During her recital she has sunk to the ground.)

JUDITH: *(Pleads.)* A tiny piece, so she won't die.

SEBASTIAN: *(Really getting angry.)* And then what? That might be just the piece we're missing. Who put the tin on the sideboard so it would be there when we ran out of food? Was that her or us? What if everyone acted the way she does? What if we acted like her? What right does she have to ask for our food, hmm? Wouldn't it be counterproductive and neglectful of us to give in to her careless pleading, wouldn't it be a thoughtless prolongation of a bad state of affairs? What kind of example would we be setting future generations and ourselves? Yes, that's right: ourselves! What's to become of us now that the apricots have run away?

JUDITH: What?

SEBASTIAN: *(Corrects himself.)* Have run out. What's to become of us now that the apricots have run out?

EVA: And in my final moments, just before it's too late and I leave a terrible impression, just before I die it suddenly no longer matters to the good in people whether I'm domestic or just foreign, because I'm finally lying on the ground and someone dashed to the ground can be reduced to the level of an animal and engender sympathy. Those are my last thoughts, then I breathe my last breath and it wafts out of me and into a statistic the good in people consumes with a piece of toast. So much for now.

(She takes her last breath.)

JUDITH: We can see she's dying but we're fine with it, aren't we?

SEBASTIAN: Fine, we already know why she's dying but we can cope with it, right?

JUDITH: Sure, and we also know that it's not her fault.

SEBASTIAN: Although we'd like to believe that it's not our fault either.

JUDITH: On the whole one could say: we're fine, aren't we?

SEBASTIAN: Sure, we're just fine.

JUDITH: Good. Very good. Are there any apricots –

SEBASTIAN: *(Looks in the tin.)* A bit of juice.

(JUDITH finishes the juice, SEBASTIAN drags EVA offstage to the right.)

SEBASTIAN: If you ask me she's making a fuss, she's so heavy she obviously still has some reserves.

JUDITH: At the end, when the lights come on again, everyone is back. And someone always feels responsible and clears away a chair that was knocked over in the final skirmish, someone makes a show of picking up this chair and clearing it away so none of his colleagues will trip over it, his dear colleagues, who are now coming back, just now you were stabbing them with a knife but now you're suddenly friends again, and it's so nice to show that, since there are lots of people watching and they like it when you clear away a chair for your colleagues. And you take each others' hands and then you're tired, terribly tired, and you're breathing heavily because you've given everything, your all, and it's so nice when you can hold your sweaty face into the light so everyone can see how exhausted you are, and the sweat drips downs from the ends of your hair because you've just given everything.

(SEBASTIAN enters from the right, he's naked, dries himself with a towel.)

SEBASTIAN: You know what I've just realised?

JUDITH: You've realised something?

SEBASTIAN: None of this is real. All this junk surrounding us isn't real.

JUDITH: Don't you want to put some clothes on?

SEBASTIAN: No. We're sitting in a cave.

JUDITH: Aha, a cave, that sounds fascinating, explain it to me.

SEBASTIAN: We're sitting in a cave and we're staring at the wall, and there are shadows dancing across it from a ray of light that falls in through the cave entrance from the outside. But we've never been out there. We're merely seeing the shadows of the great, wide, real world that lies beyond the cave.

JUDITH: You mean Plato.

SEBASTIAN: No, what I mean is: we've never actually seen the world. Our perception is pathetic. The only thing we see is the shadow of reality –

JUDITH: Yes. That's Plato. The allegory of the cave.

SEBASTIAN: Why do you keep saying Plato?

JUDITH: This theory already exists. It's by Plato.

SEBASTIAN: Yeah, right, Plato.

JUDITH: That was over two thousand years ago. But today you walk down the street and see people pushing prams and buying organic salad, and at night you put the children to bed and sing a song and somehow that makes the world round, the starry sky closes above and the space probes travelling to distant planets stay outside and I think this is the world, but then I turn on the television and suddenly the world is moving, houses are falling down and those that survive get shot because there's a war somewhere, because there are lots and lots of weapons of mass destruction stored below ground, and in another part of the world or on another channel there's a jungle and that's where the two-toed sloth lives, does he belong in this world as well now, does he eat organic salad as well, but no, he's heading for extinction and the salad isn't organic at all, it's a lie, it's poisoned, and there are no weapons of mass destruction stored below ground, it's a lie, the camps of mass destruction are above ground and under the earth there's just the smacking, swashing oil, so I quickly turn off the television and head for the slopes, they're meant to be part of the world as well, but maybe I'll break a leg there but actually if you fall you still have two lives left and when they're gone you restart the programme because my leg and the pain in my leg are just a flicker in my synapses, there is no pain, there's not even a leg because it's all, all lies, all of it, because God himself is a liar, he's not dead and he hasn't gone to take a leak but he lies like nobody's business and the world is not an object, it's merely information about an object, about an object that doesn't exist, and that's what matters, outside your cave there's nothing, you still think we should leave the cave because out there is a true, real truth waiting to be discovered but there's nothing, there is no truth, the truth doesn't exist, it never existed, it never even entered this world because the world it could have entered into doesn't exist.

(SEBASTIAN looks at her.)

SEBASTIAN: What's with the two toed sloth?

JUDITH: It doesn't exist.

(SEBASTIAN looks at her.)

SEBASTIAN: Fine. Okay. So the sloth doesn't exist. I can live with that if I have to, but –

JUDITH: No two toed sloth. No jungle.

SEBASTIAN: Okay, okay, but what about me? What about me, if there is no sloth?

JUDITH: About you?

SEBASTIAN: Yes, of course about me, who else would I be talking about?

JUDITH: You're nothing.

SEBASTIAN: What do you mean nothing?

JUDITH: You don't exist.

SEBASTIAN: But you can see me. I'm standing here.

JUDITH: You're just a flicker in my synapses.

(ROBERT enters with two suitcases. He's dressed in the same clothes he was wearing at the beginning of the play.)

ROBERT: *(Gets a fright.)* Jesus, Christ Almighty!

SEBASTIAN: *(To JUDITH.)* You're telling me straight to my face: Sebastian, you don't exist.

JUDITH: Don't take it personally.

SEBASTIAN: How else am I supposed to take it, this is about me as a person.

JUDITH: No it's not. You as a person don't exist.

ROBERT: What are you doing?

SEBASTIAN: *(To JUDITH.)* But you do? You exist, or what, eh?

JUDITH: From my point of view it looks like it, yes.

SEBASTIAN: But you're not sure?

ROBERT: Excuse me?

JUDITH: Measured against the time we didn't exist before our birth and the time we won't exist after our death, the question of our existence is completely irrelevant anyway.

ROBERT: Hello?

SEBASTIAN: I could sock you one because I exist.

JUDITH: Oh really? Says who?

SEBASTIAN: I do.

JUDITH: Doesn't exist.

SEBASTIAN: Then you'd feel pretty clearly that you exist as well.

JUDITH: It wouldn't change anything. It's just a flicker in our synapses.

ROBERT: I hate to disturb you, but the holidays are over.

SEBASTIAN: What do you want? We're in the middle of a conversation.

ROBERT: I can see that.

SEBASTIAN: *(To JUDITH.)* You see? He can see us.

JUDITH: We're merely electricity in his head: flicker, flicker.

ROBERT: The holidays are over and I'd like to sort through the mail with Eva.

SEBASTIAN: Eva's not here.

JUDITH: You see, you said it yourself: Eva doesn't exist.

SEBASTIAN: Of course she exists. She's outside getting changed.

(EVA enters from the left, she's dressed in the same clothes she was wearing at the beginning of the play. She's carrying the large potted plant.)

EVA: What did you say?

SEBASTIAN: You see, there she is.

EVA: Oh.

JUDITH: Flicker, flicker.

ROBERT: *(To EVA.)* In a minute, Eva, just a moment.

(EVA nods and disappears.)

ROBERT: *(To JUDITH and SEBASTIAN.)* It was really nice of you to empty our letterbox while we wedeled down the slopes of Niederoberaubergtal, thank you, but we're back now.

SEBASTIAN: *(Triumphant.)* Aha! Did you hear that? He's claiming he's here.

JUDITH: But he's not. That's merely human egocentricity.

ROBERT: This was meant to be a two-character scene with Eva.

(SEBASTIAN and JUDITH look at him.)

But that's fine: you can stay, I'll start going through the mail next and then I'll open the parcel.

SEBASTIAN: You're not really going to open the parcel, are you?

ROBERT: Yes. That's what it says in the text.

SEBASTIAN: Listen, Judith, we should go, he's going to open the parcel.

JUDITH: What parcel?

SEBASTIAN: *(Aghast.)* The parcel, Judith, which hasn't been opened all evening, I mean, really –

JUDITH: There is no parcel. Flicker, flicker.

SEBASTIAN: There it is, for God's sake!

JUDITH: This?

SEBASTIAN: Yes.

JUDITH: He's not going to open it, is he?

SEBASTIAN: That's what he just said.

JUDITH: *(To ROBERT.)* Don't do it, please.

ROBERT: Why? It's addressed to me.

JUDITH: Exactly. Don't open it, please.

ROBERT: I don't get it.

SEBASTIAN: Doesn't matter. Just leave it alone.

ROBERT: No, that's too vague for me, I'm going to open it.

(Picks up the parcel.)

JUDITH: Don't!

ROBERT: What?

SEBASTIAN: If you open the parcel, everything will change.

ROBERT: You have to admit that sounds a bit hysterical.

JUDITH: Trust us.

ROBERT: I can only trust in what I can see with my own eyes, seeing as everything, everything is a lie. And in any case, I might want everything to be different. That's what it says on books as well: this book will change your life. Lots of people want that, you know, that their lives are changed.

JUDITH: All right, we're leaving. He's gone mad.

SEBASTIAN: *(To JUDITH.)* Obviously.

(To ROBERT.) But don't come running to us later complaining that we didn't warn you.

JUDITH: Come on, let's go, out of this cave.

ROBERT: What's wrong with you? It's just a parcel.

SEBASTIAN: *(Dismissive gesture.)* Whatever.

(SEBASTIAN and JUDITH leave.)

ROBERT: And, er, Sebastian.

SEBASTIAN: What is it now?

ROBERT: You're not wearing anything.

SEBASTIAN: For God's sake, I know that.

(They've gone. ROBERT sits down holding the parcel. He opens it, looks inside for a long time. Takes out a letter, opens it and reads.)

ROBERT: Eva?

(Nothing.)

Eva, I opened the parcel.

(Nothing.)

Will you come here please?

(Nothing.)

Eva?

(Nothing.)

Eva, I –

(Nothing.)

I'm drawing a blank.

(Nothing. ROBERT sits, looks in the parcel, looks around helplessly. EVA enters from the kitchen. She's holding the rather large potted plant.)

EVA: What did you say?

ROBERT: I don't know – I – I don't know what comes next.

(EVA looks at him.)

EVA: Did you put this thing in the kitchen?

ROBERT: Me? You're the botanical one.

EVA: I've never seen it before.

ROBERT: You probably planted some kind of pip and while we were on holiday it put down roots and grew this plant.

EVA: No.

(Nothing.)

So. What's in the parcel?

ROBERT: I just opened it and there's a letter inside: 'Dear Mrs Eckels.'

EVA: That's me.

ROBERT: Exactly.

EVA: The parcel is for me.

ROBERT: That's beside the point for the time being. 'Dear Mrs Eckels. I have abducted your husband.'

EVA: But –

ROBERT: I know, your husband is sitting in front of you reading this letter, but – anyway: 'I have abducted your husband. If you want to get him back alive, you will obey the following instructions: become a good person. Close your accounts and help develop the development of a developing country. A joke. You can remain a bad person for all I care, but you'd better transfer the money to the account listed below. As proof that your husband is in my power, I'm enclosing a severed limb that's easily recognisable as your husband's. Yours sincerely, Eva Eckels.'

EVA: Eva Eckels?

ROBERT: Yes. Strange, isn't it.

EVA: Let me have a look.

(She takes the letter from him.)

'Eva Eckels'. That's me.

ROBERT: Exactly.

EVA: They forged me.

ROBERT: That's clearly your handwriting.

EVA: Right. That's clearly my handwriting, which is very difficult to forge because I'm extremely special and –

ROBERT: *(Interrupts her.)* Eva. I'm really worried.

EVA: Don't worry, Robert, they didn't abduct you, you're sitting here, in front of me.

ROBERT: I don't know.

EVA: They can claim whatever they want.

ROBERT: Eva, the parcel.

EVA: What about it?

ROBERT: In the parcel –

(ROBERT starts to tremble. EVA suddenly remembers.)

EVA: The severed limb.

(ROBERT nods. EVA lifts a severed head from the parcel. It's clearly ROBERT's head.)

EVA: That's your head.

ROBERT: Yes.

EVA: That's terrible. They cut your head off.

ROBERT: Looks like it. Yes.

EVA: But –

ROBERT: I know what you're thinking. The letter said: if you want to get him back alive –

EVA: Exactly. Alive. How is that going to work? Without a head.

ROBERT: Eva. I feel really unsettled.

EVA: Robert, you're not dead.

ROBERT: I don't know.

EVA: I didn't cut your head off.

ROBERT: I don't know. Maybe you'd better transfer the money. Or become a good person. Or whatever.

EVA: Robert, above all, don't hang your head.

ROBERT: Hang my what?

EVA: Whatever you do, don't lose your head.

ROBERT: Apparently I already have.

EVA: Put that out of your head.

ROBERT: Out of which one?

EVA: Why would it enter their heads to blackmail us, I can't get my head round it –

ROBERT: *(Listens.)* Eva –

EVA: Although I've got a head on my shoulders I can't make head or tail of it, we barely manage to keep our heads above water, as soon as we have some money we spend it, so let's not rack our brains about it, they're in over their heads, chin up, I won't lose my head.

ROBERT: There!

EVA: What?

ROBERT: Did you hear that?

EVA: What? I can't hear anything.

ROBERT: I think there's someone here.

EVA: Where?

ROBERT: There. Behind the wall.

EVA: Your kidnappers?

ROBERT: Listen, maybe they're already here.

EVA: In our flat?

ROBERT: I've had this feeling all night: I say something and suddenly it's as if someone is listening. Do you know what I mean?

EVA: Absolutely. Those are the normal symptoms of a psychological breakdown.

ROBERT: They're looking at us, I can feel it, now, at this very moment dozens of pairs of eyes are trained on us, can't you feel it?

EVA: But there's nothing to see.

ROBERT: They're spying on us, they're looking deep inside us like we're made of glass, and then they know what kind of people we are.

EVA: And then?

ROBERT: I don't know. Maybe they'll sell us a hoover.

EVA: *(Utterly horrified.)* What?!

ROBERT: Yes, or they'll make us put up a white gazebo tent in the garden like everyone else.

EVA: But Robert, I can't see anyone.

ROBERT: I can hear them breathing somewhere over there.

(He points in the direction of the fourth wall.)

EVA: But there's a wall there.

ROBERT: Really? You can see a wall?

EVA: You can't?

(ROBERT looks.)

Robert, you scare me when you act like this.

ROBERT: Sometimes I feel like someone is sitting out there watching us.

EVA: In our garden?

ROBERT: Yes, but now it's a big hall and they've even put up chairs so they're more comfortable.

(EVA walks towards the fourth wall.)

EVA: All I can see is a wall. But we could pretend that there's a window there and then we can look out, and if there's someone in our garden who has put a chair there in order to look into your head –

ROBERT: *(Whispering.)* Don't! Don't talk to them.

EVA: What?

ROBERT: *(Whispering.)* Maybe they don't like it if you talk to them.

EVA: *(Whispering as well now.)* No? Why not?

ROBERT: *(Whispering.)* Maybe they don't want to be disturbed while they're watching.

EVA: *(Whispering.)* Robert, you know what?

ROBERT: *(Whispering.)* Yes?

EVA: *(Whispering.)* Why are you whispering?

ROBERT: *(Whispering.)* Or we could talk in code.

(Normal volume, points at the potted plant.) Ghoscent dee crunn swisheroll, fledu bagtu escamp chupter shabring, pimk zulp contrue tripolour, wakty nitzit wull brokeof craponoun.

EVA: *(Nods.)* Aha.

ROBERT: Pintlungy plue kapper pneu, sheelifs vah blamue mah sheltopusik.

EVA: *(Nods.)* I see. And you're sure you haven't gone completely and utterly insane?

(ROBERT looks at the audience. SEBASTIAN enters as a stage hand, goes towards the coffee table, clears it and carries it offstage.)

EVA: What was that?

ROBERT: No idea.

EVA: Is it starting?

ROBERT: What?

EVA: Was that one of them?

(SEBASTIAN returns. Takes the potted plant.)

SEBASTIAN: Is this yours?

EVA: No. Yours?

SEBASTIAN: So it can go?

EVA: Er –

ROBERT: Yes. It can go.

(SEBASTIAN carries the potted plant offstage.)

ROBERT: That thing can go, can't it?

EVA: Robert. What's he doing?

ROBERT: Why don't you ask him. I've never seen him before.

(Part of the back wall crashes into the room. SEBASTIAN returns through the gap. He's carrying a cordless screwdriver and starts to dismantle the set. ROBERT and EVA watch him, utterly shocked.)

EVA: You. What are you doing?

SEBASTIAN: Taking it down.

EVA: Not now.

SEBASTIAN: Why not?

EVA: We're not finished.

SEBASTIAN: I've got my orders.

EVA: From whom?

SEBASTIAN: From above.

EVA: Oh really?

SEBASTIAN: *(To ROBERT.)* Are you on a break or can you give me a hand?

ROBERT: Where?

SEBASTIAN: If you could grab –

(ROBERT helps SEBASTIAN carry part of the set offstage, returns as a stage hand.)

EVA: But you can't just –

ROBERT: Maybe you should move the head, it's fragile. We don't want anything to fall on it.

(EVA puts the head under her arm.)

EVA: No way. This is not what we agreed on. They said we had until ten.

(To the audience.) Can someone please do something?

SEBASTIAN: I don't know anything about that. All I know is that we're supposed to clear this away.

EVA: Can someone please explain this to me? Why are they suddenly taking everything away in the middle of a scene?

ROBERT: Listen, Eva, this happens in every other German production. At the end of the play the set is taken down, you have the empty stage, radical, everything's gone, the curtain goes down, it's an old directing trick.

EVA: But this is not a German production and it's not the end of the play and I don't know anything about this.

(JUDITH enters as an assistant director.)

JUDITH: Sorry Eva, I should have told you –

EVA: Told me what? I don't believe this, they're barging right into my scene, is this how you do things around here?

SEBASTIAN: Could we have the workers on, please?

ROBERT: It's really dark back here.

EVA: Listen to this, they're shouting as if all this was theirs, as if all this was about the technicians, not art.

JUDITH: Eva, I have something to tell you –

EVA: I've never experienced anything like this in any other theatre.

JUDITH: Eva, he doesn't like the set anymore.

EVA: What do you mean, he doesn't like the set anymore? Has he lost his mind?

JUDITH: He said that if he has to spend another minute looking at this set he's going to puke into the next row.

EVA: Then he should tell me, fucking hell, but not have it taken away in the middle of my scene, right from underneath me –

JUDITH: I know, I don't think it's a good way to behave either, but all he said was: out, out, throw this crap out, and that it's a lot better to do it on an empty stage and that everything needs to be much more radical, more simple, more abstract and not so obviously psychological –

EVA: That's what I said right from the beginning, we can't do it on this set, but he should have thought of that sooner, where is he anyway –

JUDITH: He left.

EVA: He what?

JUDITH: He went away.

EVA: Where? To the canteen?

JUDITH: Home. I think he went home.

EVA: I don't believe this.

JUDITH: He said the whole thing makes him sick and he doesn't want anything to do with it anymore.

EVA: But I'm here. I'm giving it my all –

SEBASTIAN: *(Working.)* Well – you haven't given that much.

JUDITH: To be honest –

EVA: What?

JUDITH: To be honest he hasn't been here today.

EVA: What, he didn't even show up?

JUDITH: Actually I haven't seen him in rehearsals for several days.

EVA: What?

JUDITH: I think he's having some kind of breakdown.

EVA: You're telling me we've spent the past couple of days rehearsing without a director?

JUDITH: Actually I don't think he's been here since we started.

EVA: You mean not at all? In the sense of 'never'?

SEBASTIAN: *(Referring to a piece of set he's carrying.)* Does anyone know where this is supposed to go?

JUDITH: *(To SEBASTIAN.)* No idea.

(SEBASTIAN carries it offstage.)

JUDITH: *(To EVA.)* I don't think he ever showed up here, in the theatre.

EVA: In that case what are we doing here?

JUDITH: Sometimes I feel like there is no director.

ROBERT: *(Referring to a piece of set he's carrying.)* What about this one?

JUDITH: Listen, just put it down somewhere. We don't know either.

EVA: There's no director?

JUDITH: That's my feeling. I think it was just a thought to reassure us.

ROBERT: We're going to have a break as well now, okay?

JUDITH: Yeah, sure, have a break.

ROBERT: Do you want a beer?

(He opens bottles for EVA and JUDITH.)

JUDITH: Thanks.

(ROBERT sits down and drinks beer. JUDITH sits down as well and drinks. EVA has remained standing.)

JUDITH: The other day I met Friedrich in the corridor, and Friedrich thinks he's dead.

EVA: Dead?

(SEBASTIAN enters wearing a Nietzsche beard.)

SEBASTIAN: Where is he gone? I mean to tell you! We have killed him, – you and I! We are all his murderers! But how have we done it? How were we able to drink up the sea? Who gave us the sponge to wipe away the whole horizon? What did we do when we loosened this earth from its sun?

Whither does it now move? Whither do we move? Away from all suns? Do we not dash on unceasingly? Backwards, sideways, forewards, in all directions? Is there still an above and below? Do we not stray, as through infinite nothingness? Does not empty space breathe upon us? Has it not become colder? Does not night come on continually, darker and darker? Shall we not have to light lanterns in the morning? Do we not hear the noise of the grave-diggers who are burying him? Do we not smell his putrefaction? – for even he putrefies! He is dead! He remains dead! And we have killed him![1]

(SEBASTIAN falls off the back of the stage.)

EVA: What do you mean, dead?

JUDITH: I got a bit of a fright at first as well.

EVA: Dead, Friedrich is talking nonsense, why doesn't he start by taking that awful beard off.

JUDITH: But I don't think it's true either, because if he was dead that means that once upon a time he existed.

EVA: And you think –

JUDITH: My feeling is, that this was going on without him right from the beginning.

EVA: So there is no director.

JUDITH: No.

EVA: There's never been one.

JUDITH: No, or it wouldn't look like this, would it.

EVA: Hmm.

JUDITH: Sit down and have a drink.

(EVA sits down and drinks.)

EVA: But I always thought there's someone out there watching me.

JUDITH: Well.

(EVA stares in the direction of the audience. SEBASTIAN has returned with a beer bottle and joins them.)

SEBASTIAN: What's wrong with her – ?

ROBERT: Shock.

SEBASTIAN: That's what shock looks like?

ROBERT: No, in real life it's different, she's only acting.

EVA: *(To the audience.)* Hello? Is someone there?

JUDITH: Don't. It's quite nice like this, don't you think?

(EVA listens and looks around.)

JUDITH: Look, everything carries on anyway. Everything always carries on. The music is playing. The floodlights are on. Somewhere someone is talking. It never stops.

SEBASTIAN: But we do have to call it a day at some point.

JUDITH: But we still have lots of time till then. And no one shouts at you and tells you all the things you're doing wrong. You can do whatever you want.

EVA: That's true. It's nice.

(Nothing.)

I'm just wondering: so who cast me?

(Nothing.)

SEBASTIAN: Are we done?

ROBERT: Not yet.

JUDITH: *(To ROBERT.)* Are you going to do your announcement?

(ROBERT stands up.)

ROBERT: Taw biba shin blowument, pontery poudly sny binnie frabill. Onka elmy spraysa bleam, onna tetherloot ilshwater brakebock. And now, to conclude, a song:

JUDITH, ROBERT, SEBASTIAN and EVA: *(Sing.)*

Go to sleep, my little star,
Wonder where your parents are?
Sleep, they have just gone from here,
Sleep, my child, no need to fear,
Sleep, so you won't realise.

Sleep like you're in paradise.

Go to sleep, my little star,
Wonder where the people are?
Sleep, there's no one in this place,
An abandoned empty space.
Sleep, so you won't realise.
Sleep like you're in paradise.

Go to sleep, my little star,
Do you wonder where we are?
Sleep, we're nothing but a dream
And will soon dissolve in steam.
Our existence is disguise.
Sleep like you're in paradise.

The End

1 *The Joyful Wisdom*, translated by Thomas Common, in *The Complete Works of Friedrich Nietzsche. The First Complete Authorized English Translation.* Edited by Oscar Levy, 18 vols., Edinburgh and London, T.N. Foulis, 1909-1913

www.ingramcontent.com/pod-product-compliance
Ingram Content Group UK Ltd.
Pitfield, Milton Keynes, MK11 3LW, UK
UKHW020710030325
455689UK00009BA/178

9 781783 199433